Towards the Great Peace

Ralph Adams Cram

Contents

- INTRODUCTION 7
- I A WORLD AT THE CROSSROADS 9
- II A WORKING PHILOSOPHY 27
- III THE SOCIAL ORGANISM 42
- IV THE INDUSTRIAL PROBLEM 61
- V THE POLITICAL ORGANIZATION OF SOCIETY 83
- VI THE FUNCTION OF EDUCATION AND ART 103
- VII THE PROBLEM OF ORGANIC RELIGION 124
- VIII PERSONAL RESPONSIBILITY 144

TOWARDS THE GREAT PEACE

BY
Ralph Adams Cram

INTRODUCTION

For the course of lectures I am privileged to deliver at this time, I desire to take, in some sense as a text, a prayer that came to my attention at the outset of my preparatory work. It is adapted from a prayer by Bishop Hacket who flourished about the middle of the seventeenth century, and is as follows:

Lord, lift us out of Private-mindedness and give us Public
souls to work for Thy Kingdom by daily creating that Atmosphere
of a happy temper and generous heart which alone can bring the
Great Peace.

Each thought in this noble aspiration is curiously applicable to each one of us in the times in which we fall: the supersession of narrow and selfish and egotistical "private-mindedness" by a vital passion for the winning of a Kingdom of righteousness consonant with the revealed will of God; the lifting of souls from nervous introspection to a height where they become indeed "public souls"; the accomplishing of the Kingdom not by great engines of mechanical power but by the daily offices of every individual; the substitution in place of current hatred, fear and jealous covetousness, of the unhappy temper and "generous heart" which are the only fruitful agencies of accomplishment. Finally, the "Great Peace" as the supreme object of thought and act and aspiration for us, and for all the world, at this time of crisis which has culminated through the antithesis of great peace, which is great war.

I have tried to keep this prayer of Bishop Hacket's before me during the preparation of these lectures. I cannot claim that I have succeeded in achieving a "happy temper" in all things, but I honestly claim that I have striven earnestly for the "generous heart," even when forced, by what seem to me the necessities of the case, to indulge in condemnation or to bring forward subjects which can only be controversial. If the "Great War," and the greater war which preceded, comprehended, and followed it, were the result of many and varied errors, it matters little whether these were the result of perversity, bad judgment or the most generous impulses. As they resulted in the Great War, so they are a detriment to the Great Peace that must follow, and therefore they must be cast away. Consciousness of sin, repentance, and a will to do better, must precede the act of amendment, and we must see where we have erred if we are to forsake our ill ways and make an honest effort to strive for something better.

For every failure I have made to achieve either a happy temper or a generous heart, I hereby express my regret, and tender my apologies in advance.

I
A WORLD AT THE CROSSROADS

For two thousand years Christianity has been an operative force in the world; for more than a century democracy has been the controlling influence in the public affairs of Europe and the Americas; for two generations education, free, general and comprehensive, has been the rule in the West. Wealth incomparable, scientific achievements unexampled in their number and magnitude, facile means of swift intercommunication between peoples, have all worked together towards an earthly realization of the early nineteenth-century dream of proximate and unescapable millennium. With the opening of the second decade of the twentieth century it seemed that the stage was set for the last act in an unquestioned evolutionary drama. Man was master of all things, and the failures of the past were obliterated by the glory of the imminent event.

The Great War was a progressive revelation and disillusionment. Therein, everything so carefully built up during the preceding four centuries was tried as by fire, and each failed--save the indestructible qualities of personal honour, courage and fortitude. Nothing corporate, whether secular or ecclesiastical, endured the test, nothing of government or administration, of science or industry, of philosophy or religion. The victories were those of individual character, the things that stood the test were not things but ***men.***

The "War to end war," the war "to make the world safe for democracy" came to a formal ending, and for a few hours the world gazed spellbound on golden hopes. Greater than the disillusionment of war was that of the making of the peace. There had never been a war, not even the "Thirty Years' War" in Germany, the "Hundred Years' War" in France or the wars of Napoleon, that was fraught with more horror, devastation and dishonour; there had never been a Peace, not even those of Berlin,

Vienna and Westphalia, more cynical or more deeply infected with the poison of ultimate disaster. And here it was not things that failed, but *men.*

What of the world since the Peace of Versailles? Hatred, suspicion, selfishness are the dominant notes. The nations of Europe are bankrupt financially, and the governments of the world are bankrupt politically. Society is dissolving into classes and factions, either at open war or manoeuvering for position, awaiting the favourable moment. Law and order are mocked at, philosophy and religion disregarded, and of all the varied objects of human veneration so loudly acclaimed and loftily exalted by the generation that preceded the war, not one remains to command a wide allegiance. One might put it in a sentence and say that everyone is dissatisfied with everything, and is showing his feelings after varied but disquieting fashion. It is a condition of unstable equilibrium constantly tending by its very nature to a point where dissolution is apparently inevitable.

It is no part of my task to elaborate this thesis, and still less to magnify its perils. Enough has been said and written on this subject during the last two years; more than enough, perhaps, and in any case no thinking person is unaware of the conditions that exist, whatever may be his estimate of their significance, his interpenetration of their tendency. I have set myself the task of trying to suggest some constructive measures that we may employ in laying the foundations for the immediate future; they may be wrong in whole or in part, but at least my object and motive are not recrimination or invective, but regeneration. Nevertheless, as a foundation the case must be stated, and as a necessary preparation to any work that looks forward we must have at least a working hypothesis as to how the conditions that need redemption were brought about. I state the case thus, therefore: That human society, even humanity itself, is now in a state of flux that at any moment may change into a chaos comparable only with that which came with the fall of classical civilization and from which five centuries were necessary for the process of recovery. Christianity, democracy, science, education, wealth, and the cumulative inheritance of a thousand years, have not preserved us from the vain repetition of history. How has this been possible, what has been the sequence of events that has brought us to this pass?

It is of course the result of the interaction of certain physical, material facts and certain spiritual forces. Out of these spiritual energies come events, phenomena that manifest themselves in political, social, ecclesiastical transactions and institutions; in wars, migrations and the reshaping of states; in codes of law, the organization of society, the development of art, literature and science. In their turn all these concrete products work on the minds and souls of men, modifying old spiritual impulses either by exaltation or degradation, bringing new ones into play; and again these react on the material fabric of human life, causing new combinations, unloosing new forces, that in their turn play their part in the eternal process of building, unbuilding and rebuilding our unstable and fluctuant world.

Underlying all the varied material forms of ancient society, as this developed around the shores of the Mediterranean, was the great fact of slavery: Persia, Assyria, Babylonia, Egypt, Greece, Rome, all were small, sometimes very small, minorities of highly developed, highly privileged individuals existing on a great substratum of slaves. All the vast contributions of antiquity in government and law, in science, letters, art and philosophy, all the building of the culture and civilization that still remain the foundation stones of human society, was the work of the few free subsisting on the many un-free. But freedom, liberty, is an attribute of the soul and it may exist even when the body is in bondage. The slaves of antiquity were free neither in body nor in soul, but with the coming of Christianity all this was changed, for it is one of the great glories of the Christian religion that it gave freedom to the soul even before the Church could give freedom to the body of the slave. After the fall of the Roman Empire, and with the infiltration of the free races of the North, slavery gradually disappeared, and between the years 1000 and 1500 a very real liberty existed as the product of Christianity and under its protection. Society was hierarchical: from the serf up through the peasant, the guildsman, the burgher, the knighthood, the nobles, to the King, and so to the Emperor, there was a regular succession of graduations, but the lines of demarcation were fluid and easily passed, and as through the Church, the schools and the cloister there was an open road for the son of a peasant to achieve the Papacy, so through the guilds, chivalry, war and the court, the layman, if he possessed ability, might from an humble beginning travel far. An epoch of real liberty, of body, soul and mind, and the more real in that limits, differences and degrees were recognized, accepted and enforced.

This condition existed roughly for five centuries in its swift rise, its long dominion and its slow decline, that is to say, from 1000 A.D. to 1500 A.D. There was still the traditional aristocracy, now feudal rather than patriarchal or military; there was still a servile class, now reduced to a small minority. In between was the great body of men of a degree of character, ability and intelligence, and with a recognized status, the like of which had never been seen before. It was not a bourgeoisie, for it was made up of producers,--agricultural, artisan, craft, art, mechanic; a great free society, the proudest product of Christian civilization.

With the sixteenth century began a process of change that was to overturn all this and bring in something radically different. The Renaissance and the Reformation worked in a sense together to build up their own expressive form of society, and when this process had been completed we find still an aristocracy, though rapidly changing in the quality of its personnel and in the sense of its relationship to the rest of society; a servile class, the proletariat, enormously increased in proportion to the other social components; and two new classes, one the bourgeoisie, essentially non-producers and subsisting largely either on trade, usury or management, and the pauper, a phase of life hitherto little known under the Christian regime. The great body of free citizens that had made up the majority of society during the preceding epoch, the small land-holders, citizens, craftsmen and artists of fifty different sorts, has begun rapidly to dissolve, has almost vanished by the middle of the seventeenth century, and in another hundred years has practically disappeared.

What had become of them, of this great bulk of the population of western Europe that, with the feudal aristocracy, the knighthood and the monks had made Mediaevalism? Some had degenerated into bourgeois traders, managers and financeers, but the great majority had been crushed down and down in the mass of submerged proletariat, losing liberty, degenerating in character, becoming more and more servile in status and wretched in estate, so forming a huge, inarticulate, dully ebullient mass, cut off from society, cut off almost from life itself.

I must insist on these three factors in the development of society and its present catastrophe: the great, predominant, central body of free men during the Middle Ages, their supersession during the sixteenth, seventeenth and eighteenth centuries by a non-producing bourgeoisie, and the creation during the same period of a submerged proletariat. They are factors of great significance and potential force.

Towards the end of the eighteenth century the industrial-financial revolution began. Within the space of an hundred years came all the revelations of the potential inherent in thermo-dynamics and electricity, and the invention of the machines that have changed the world. During the Renaissance and Reformation the old social and economic systems, so laboriously built up on the ruins of Roman tyranny, had been destroyed; autocracy had abolished liberty, licentiousness had wrecked the moral stamina, "freedom of conscience" had obliterated the guiding and restraining power of the old religion. The field was clear for a new dispensation.

What happened was interesting and significant. Coal and iron, and their derivatives--steam and machinery--rapidly revealed their possibilities. To take advantage of these, it was necessary that labour should be available in large quantities and freely subject to exploitation; that unlimited capital should be forthcoming; that adequate markets should be discovered or created to absorb the surplus product, so enormously greater than the normal demand; and finally, it was necessary that directors and organizers and administrators should be ready at the call. The conditions of the time made all these possible. The land-holding peasantry of England--and it is here that the revolution was accomplished--had been largely dispossessed and pauperized under Henry VIII, Edward VI and Elizabeth, while the development of the wool-growing industry had restricted the arable land to a point where it no longer gave employment to the mass of field labourers. The first blast of factory production threw out of work the whole body of cottage weavers, smiths, craftsmen; and the result was a great mass of men, women, and children without defense, void of all rights, and given the alternative of submission to the dominance of the exploiters, or starvation.

Without capital the new industry could neither begin nor continue. The exploits of the "joint-stock companies" invented and perfected in the eighteenth century, showed how this capital could easily be obtained, while the paralyzing and dismemberment of the Church during the Reformation had resulted in the abrogation of the old ecclesiastical inhibition against usury. The necessary capital was forthcoming, and the foundations were laid for the great system of finance which was one of the triumphant achievements of the last century.

The question of markets was more difficult. It was clear that, through machinery, the exploitation of labour, and the manipulations of finance, the product would be enormously greater than the local or national demand. Until they themselves developed their own industrial system, the other nations of Europe were available, but as this process proceeded other markets had to be found; the result was achieved through advertising, i.e., the stimulating in the minds of the general public of a covetousness for something they had not known of and did not need, and the exploiting of barbarous or undeveloped races in Asia, Africa, Oceanica. This last task was easily achieved through "peaceful penetration" and the preempting of "spheres of influence." In the end (i.e., A.D. 1914), the whole world had so been divided, the stimulated markets showed signs of repletion, and since exaggerated profits meant increasing capital demanding investment, and the improvement in "labour-saving" devices continued unchecked, the contest for others' markets became acute, and world-politic was concentrated on the vital problem of markets, lines of communication, and tariffs.

As for the finding or development of competent organizers and directors, the history of the world since the end of medievalism had curiously provided for this after a fashion that seemed almost miraculous. The type required was different from anything that had been developed before. Whenever the qualitative standard had been operative, it was necessary that the leaders in any form of creative action should be men of highly developed intellect, fine sensibility, wide and penetrating vision, nobility of instinct, passion for righteousness, and a consciousness of the eternal force of charity, honour, and service. During the imperial or decadent stages, courage, dynamic force, the passion for adventure, unscrupulousness in the matter of method, took the place of the qualities that marked the earlier periods. In the first instance the result was the great law-givers, philosophers, prophets, religious leaders, and artists of every sort; in the second, the great conquerors. Something quite different was now demanded--men who possessed some of the qualities needed for the development of imperialism, but who were unhampered by the restrictive influences of those who had sought perfection. To organize and administer the new industrial-financial-commercial regime, the leaders must be shrewd, ingenious, quick-witted, thick-skinned, unscrupulous, hard-headed, and avaricious; yet daring, dominating, and gifted with keen prevision and vivid imagination. These qualities had not been bred under any of the Mediterranean civilizations, or that of Central Europe in the Middle Ages, which had inherited so much therefrom. The pursuit of perfection always implies a definite aristocracy, which is as much a goal of effort as a noble philosophy, an august civil polity or a great art. This aristocracy was an accepted and indispensable part of society, and it was always more or less the same in principle, and always the centre and source of leadership, without which society cannot endure. It is true that at the hands of Christianity it acquired a new quality, that of service as contingent on privilege--one might almost say of privilege as contingent on service--and the ideals of honour, chivalry, compassion were established as its object and method of operation even though these were not always achieved, but the result was not a new creation; it was an institution as old as society, regenerated and transformed and playing a greater and a nobler part than ever before.

Between the years 1455 and 1795 this old aristocracy was largely exterminated. The Wars of the Roses, the massacres of the Reformation, and the Civil Wars in England; the Thirty Years' War in Germany; the Hundred Years' War, the Wars of Religion, and the Revolution in France had decimated the families old in honour, preserving the tradition of culture, jealous of their alliances and their breeding--the natural and actual leaders in thought and action. England suffered badly enough as the result of war, with the persecutions of Henry VIII, Edward VI and Elizabeth, and the Black Death, included for full measure. France suffered also, but Germany fared worst of all. By the end of the Thirty Years' War the older feudal nobility had largely disappeared, while the class of "gentlemen" had been almost exterminated. In France, until the fall of Napoleon III, and in Germany and Great Britain up to the present moment, the recruiting of the formal aristocracy has gone on steadily, but on a different basis and from a different class from anything known before. Demonstrated personal ability to gain and maintain leadership; distinguished service to the nation in war or statecraft; courage, honour, fealty--these, in general, had been the ground for admission to the ranks of the aristocracy. In general, also, advancement to the ranks of the higher nobility was from the class of "gentlemen," though the Church, the universities, and chivalry gave, during the Middle Ages, wide opportunity for personal merit to achieve the highest honours.

Through the wholesale destruction of the representatives of a class that from the beginning of history had been the directing and creative force in civilization, a process began which was almost mechanical. As the upper strata of society were planed off by war, pestilence, civil slaughter, and assassination, the pressure on the great mass of men (peasants, serfs, unskilled labourers, the so-called "lower classes") was increasingly relaxed, and very soon the thin film of aristocracy, further weakened by dilution, broke, and through the crumbling shell burst to the surface those who had behind them no tradition but that of servility, no comprehension of the ideals of chivalry and honour of the gentleman, no stored-up results of education and culture, but only an age-long rage against the age-long dominating class, together with the instincts of craftiness, parsimony, and almost savage self-interest.

As a class, it was very far from being what it was under the Roman Empire; on the other hand, it was equally removed from what it was during the Middle Ages in England, France and the Rhineland. Under mediaevalism chattel slavery had disappeared, and the lot of the peasant was a happier one than he had known before. He had achieved definite status, and the line that separated him from the gentry was very thin and constantly traversed, thanks to the accepted system of land tenure, the guilds, chivalry, the schools and universities, the priesthood and monasticism. The Renaissance had rapidly changed all this, however; absolutism in government, dispossession of land, the abolition of the guilds, and the collapse of the moral order and of the dominance of the Church, were fast pushing the peasant back into the position he had held under the Roman Empire, and from which Christianity had lifted him. By 1790 he had been for nearly three centuries under a progressive oppression that had undone nearly all the beneficent work of the Middle Ages and made the peasant class practically outlaw, while breaking down its character, degrading its morals, increasing its ignorance, and building up a sullen rage and an invincible hatred of all that stood visible as law and order in the persons of the ruling class.

Filtering through the impoverished and diluted crust of a dissolving aristocracy, came this irruption from below. In their own persons certain of these people possessed the qualities and the will which were imperative for the organization of the industry, the trade, and the finance that were to control the world for four generations, and produce that industrial civilization which is the basis and the energizing force of modernism. Immediately, and with conspicuous ability, they took hold of the problem, solved its difficulties, developed its possibilities, and by the end of the nineteenth century had made it master of the world.

Simultaneously an equal revolution and reversal was being effected in government. The free monarchies of the Middle Ages, beneath which lay the well recognized principle that no authority, human or divine, could give any monarch the right to govern wrong, and that there was such a thing (frequently exercised) as lawful rebellion, gave place to the absolutism and autocracy of Renaissance kingship and this, which was fostered both by Renaissance and Reformation, became at once the ally of the new forces in society and so furthered the growth as well as the misery and the degradation of the proletariat. In revolt against this new and very evil thing came the republicanism of the eighteenth century, inspired and directed in large measure by members of the fast perishing aristocracy of race, character and tradition. It was a splendid uprising against tyranny and oppression and is best expressed in the personalities and the actions of the Constitutional Convention of the United States in 1787 and the States General of France in 1789.

The movement is not to be confounded with another that synchronizes with it, that is to say, democracy, for the two things are radically different in their antecedents, their protagonists, their modes of operation and their objects. While the one was the aspiration and the creation of the more enlightened and cultured, the representatives of the old aristocracy, the other issued out of the same ***milieu*** that was responsible for the new social organism. That is to say; while certain of the more shrewd and ingenious were organizing trade, manufacture and finance and developing its autocratic and imperialistic possibilities at the expense of the great mass of their blood-brothers, others of the same social antecedents were devising a new theory, and experimenting in new schemes, of government, which would take all power away from the class that had hitherto exercised it and fix it firmly in the hands of the emancipated proletariat. This new model was called then, and is called now, democracy. Elsewhere I have tried to distinguish between democracy of theory and democracy of method. Perhaps I should have used a more lucid nomenclature if I had simply distinguished between republicanism and democracy, for this is what it amounts to. The former is as old as man, and is part of the "passion for perfection" that characterizes all crescent society, and is indeed the chief difference between brute and human nature; it means the guaranteeing of justice, and may be described as consisting of abolition of privilege, equality of opportunity, and utilization of ability. Democracy of method consists in a variable and uncertain sequence of devices which are supposed to achieve the democracy of ideal, but as a matter of fact have thus far usually worked in the opposite direction. The activity of this movement synchronizes with the pressing upward of the "the masses" through the dissolving crust of "the classes," and represents their contribution to the science of political philosophy, as the contribution of the latter is current "political economy."

It will be perceived that the reaction of the new social force in the case of industrial organization is fundamentally opposed to that which occurred in the political sphere. The one is working steadily towards an autocratic imperialism and the "servile state," the other towards the fluctuating, incoherent control of the making and administering of laws by the untrained, the uncultivated, and the generally unfit, the issue of which is anarchy. The industrial-commercial-financial oligarchy that dominated society for the century preceding the Great War is the result of the first; Russia, today, is an exemplar of the second. The working out of these two great devices of the new force released by the destructive processes of the sixteenth, seventeenth, and eighteenth centuries, simultaneously though in apparent opposition, explains why, when the war broke out, imperialism and democracy synchronized so exactly: on the one hand, imperial states, industry, commerce, and finance; on the other, a swiftly accelerating democratic system that was at the same time the effective means whereby the dominant imperialism worked, and the omnipresent and increasing threat to its further continuance.

A full century elapsed before victory became secure, or even proximate. Republicanism rapidly extended itself to all the governments of western Europe, but it could not maintain itself in its primal integrity. Sooner here, later there, it surrendered to the financial, industrial, commercial forces that were taking over the control and direction of society, becoming partners with them and following their aims, conniving at their schemes, and sharing in their ever-increasing profits. By the end of the first decade of the twentieth century these supposedly "free" governments had become as identified with "special privilege," and as widely severed from the people as a whole, as the autocratic governments of the seventeenth and eighteenth centuries, while they failed consistently to match them in effectiveness, energy and efficiency of operation.

For this latter condition democracy was measurably responsible. For fifty years it had been slowly filtering into the moribund republican system until at last, during the same first decade of the present century, it had wholly transformed the governmental system, making it, whatever its outward form, whether constitutional monarchy, or republic, essentially democratic. So government became shifty, opportunist, incapable, and without the inherent energy to resist, beyond a certain point, the last great effort of the emergent proletariat to destroy, not alone the industrial civilization it justly detested, but the very government it had acquired by "peaceful penetration" and organized and administered along its chosen lines, and indeed the very fabric of society itself.

Now these two remarkable products of the new mentality of a social force were facts, but they needed an intellectual or philosophical justification just as a lowborn profiteer, when he has acquired a certain amount of money, needs an expensive club or a coat of arms to regularize his status. Protestantism and materialistic philosophy were joint nursing-mothers to modernism, but when, by the middle of the last century, it had reached man's estate, they proved inadequate; something else was necessary, and this was furnished to admiration by evolutionism. Through its doctrine of the survival of the fittest, it appeared to justify in the fullest degree the gospel of force as the final test, and "enlightened self-interest" as the new moral law; through its lucid demonstration of the strictly physical basis of life, the "descent of man" from primordial slime by way of the lemur or the anthropoid ape, and the non-existence of any supernatural power that had devised, or could determine, a code of morality in which certain things were eternal by right, and other than the variable reactions of very highly developed animals to experience and environment, it had given weighty support to the increasingly popular movement towards democracy both in theory and in act.

Its greatest contribution, however, was its argument that, since the invariable law of life was one of progressive evolution, therefore the acquired characteristics which formed the material of evolution, and were heritable, could be mechanically increased in number by education; hence the body of inheritance (which unfortunately varied as between man and man because of past discrepancies in environment, opportunities, and education) could be equalized by a system of teaching that aimed to furnish that mental and physical training hitherto absent.

Whether the case was ever so stated in set terms does not matter; very shortly this became the firm conviction of the great mass of men, and the modern democracy of method is based on the belief that all men are equal because they are men, and that free, compulsory, secularized, state-controlled education can and does remove the last difference that made possible any discrimination in rights and privileges as between one man and another.

In another respect, however, the superstition of mechanical evolution played an important part, and with serious results. Neither the prophets nor the camp-followers seemed to realize that evolution, while undoubtedly a law of life within certain limits, was inseparable from degradation which was its concomitant, that is to say, that as the rocket rises so must it fall; as man is conceived, born and matures, even so must he die. The wave rises, but falls again; the state waxes to greatness, wanes, and the map knows it no more; each epoch of human history arises out of dim beginnings, magnifies itself in glory, and then yields to internal corruption, dilution and adulteration of blood, or prodigal dissipation of spiritual force, and takes its place in the annals of ancient history. Without recognition of this implacable, unescapable fact of degradation sequent on evolution, the later becomes a delusion and an instrument of death, for the eyes of man are blind to incipient or crescent dangers; content, self-secure, lost in a vain dream of manifest destiny they are deaf to warnings, incapable even of the primary gestures of self-defense. Such was one of the results of nineteenth-century evolutionism, and the generation that saw the last years of the nineteenth century and the first part of the new, basking in its day dreams of self-complacency, made no move to avert the dangers that threatened it then and now menace it with destruction.

When, therefore, modernism achieved its grand climacteric in July, 1914, we had on the one hand an imperialism of force, in industry, commerce, and finance, expressing itself through highly developed specialists, and dictating the policies and practices of government, society, and education; on the other, a democracy of form which denied, combated, and destroyed distinction in personality and authority in thought, and discouraged constructive leadership in the intellectual, spiritual, and artistic spheres of activity. The opposition was absolute, the results catastrophic. The lack of competent leadership in every category of life finds a sufficient explanation in the two opposed forces, in their origin and nature, and in the fact of their opposition.

In the somewhat garish light of the War and the Peace, it would not be difficult to feel a real and even poignant sympathy for two causes that were prominent and popular in the first fourteen years of the present century, namely, the philosophy that based itself on a mechanical system of evolution which predicted unescapable, irreversible human progress, and that religion which denied the reality of evil in the world. The plausibility of each was dissipated by the catastrophic events though both still linger in stubborn unconsciousness of their demise. The impulse towards sympathy is mitigated by realization of the unfortunate effect they exerted on history. This is particularly true of evolutionary philosophy, which was held as an article of faith, either consciously or sub-consciously, by the greater part of Western society. Not only did it deter men from realizing the ominous tendency of events but, more unhappily, it minimized their power to discriminate between what was good and bad in current society, and even reversed their sense of comparative values. If man was indeed progressing steadily from bad to good, and so to better and best, then the vivid and even splendid life of the last quarter of the nineteenth century, with its headlong conquest of the powers of nature, its enormous industrial development, its vast and ever-increasing wealth in material things, must be not only an amazing advance beyond any former civilization but positively good in itself, while the future could only be a progressive magnifying of what then was going on. "Just as" to quote Mr. Chesterton's admirable Dr. Pelkins, "just as when we see a pig in a litter larger than the other pigs, we know that by an unalterable law of the Inscrutable, it will some day be larger than an elephant...so we know and reverently acknowledge that when any power in human politics has shown for any period of time any considerable activity, it will go on until it reaches the sky."

Nothing but a grave inability to estimate values, based on a pseudo-scientific dogma, can explain the lack of any just standard of comparative values that was the essential quality in pre-war society. Extraordinary as were the material achievements of the time, beneficent in certain ways, and susceptible in part of sometime being used to the advantage of humanity, they were largely negatived, and even reversed in value, just because the sense of proportion had been lost. The image which might have stimulated reverence had become a fetish. There were voices crying in the wilderness against a worship that had poisoned into idolatry, but they were unheard. Progressively the real things of life were blurred and forgotten and the things that were so obviously real that they were unreal became the object and the measure of achievement.

It was an unhappy and almost fatal attitude of mind, and it was engendered not so much by the trend of civilization since the Renaissance and Reformation, nor by the compulsion and cumulative influence of the things themselves, as by the natural temper and inclinations and the native standards of this emancipated mass of humanity that, oppressed, outraged and degraded for four hundred years had at last burst out of its prison-house and had assumed control of society through industrialism, politics and social life. The saving grace of the old aristocracies had disappeared with the institution itself: between 1875 and 1900 the great single leaders, so fine in character, so brilliant in capacity, so surprising in their numbers, that had given a deceptive glory to the so-called Victorian Age, had almost wholly died out, and the new conditions neither fostered the development of adequate successors, nor gave audience to the few that, anomalously, appeared. It is not surprising therefore that the new social element that had played so masterly a part in bringing to its perfection the industrial-financial-democratic scheme of life should have developed an apologetic therefor, and imposed it, with all its materialism, its narrowness, its pragmatism, its, at times, grossness and cynicism, on the mind of a society where increasingly their own followers were, by sheer energy and efficiency, acquiring a predominant position.

I am not unconscious that these are hard sayings and that few indeed will accept them. They seem too much like attempting that which Burke said was impossible, viz., to bring an indictment against a people. I intend nothing of the sort. Out of this same body of humanity which **as a whole** has exerted this very unfavourable influence on modern society, have come and will come personalities of sudden and startling nobility, men who have done as great service as any of their contemporaries whatever their class or status. Out of the depths have come those who have ascended to the supreme heights, for since Christianity came into the world to free the souls of men, this new liberty has worked without limitations of caste or race. Indeed, the very creations of the emergent force, industrialism and democracy, while they were the betrayal of the many were the opportunity of the few, taking the place, as they did, of the older creeds of specifically Christian society, and inviting those who would to work their full emancipation and so become the servants of God and mankind. By the very bitterness of their antecedents, the cruelty of their inheritance, they gained a deeper sense of the reality of life, a more just sense of right and wrong, a clearer vision of things as they were, than happened in the case of those who had no such experience of the deep brutality of the regime of post-Renaissance society.

True as this is, it is also true that for one who won through there were many who gained nothing, and it was, and is, the sheer weight of numbers of those who failed of this that has made their influence on the modern life as pervasive and controlling as it is.

What has happened is a certain degradation of character, a weakening of the moral stamina of men, and against this no mechanical device in government, no philosophical or social theory, can stand a chance of successful resistance, while material progress in wealth and trade and scientific achievement becomes simply a contributory force in the process of degeneration. For this degradation of character we are bound to hold this new social force in a measure responsible, even though it has so operated because of its inherent qualities and in no material respect through conscious cynicism or viciousness; indeed it is safe to say that in so far as it was acting consciously it was with good motives, which adds an element of even greater tragedy to a situation already sufficiently depressing.

If I am right in holding this to be the effective cause of the situation we have now to meet, it is true that it is by no means the only one. The emancipation and deliverance of the downtrodden masses of men who owed their evil estate to the destruction of the Christian society of the Middle Ages, was a clamourous necessity; it was a slavery as bad in some ways as any that had existed in antiquity, and the number of its victims was greater. The ill results of the accomplished fact was largely due to the condition of religion which existed during the period of emancipation. No society can endure without vital religion, and any revolution effected at a time when religion is moribund or dissipated in contentious fragments, is destined to be evacuated of its ideals and its potential, and to end in disaster. Now the freeing of the slaves of the Renaissance and the post-Reformation, and their absorption in the body politic, was one of the greatest revolutions in history, and it came at a time when religion, which had been one and vital throughout Western Europe for six centuries, had been shattered and nullified, and its place taken, in the lands that saw the great liberation, by Calvinism, Lutheranism, Puritanism and atheism, none of which could exert a guiding and redemptive influence on the dazed hordes that had at last come up into the light of day.

In point of fact, therefore, we are bound to trace back the responsibility for the present crisis even to the Reformation itself, as well as to the tyranny and absolutism of government, and the sordid and profligate ordering of society, which followed on the end of Mediaevalism.

So then we stand today confronting a situation that is ominous and obscure, since the very ideals and devices which we had held were the last word in progressive evolution have failed at the crisis, and because we who created them and have worked through them, have failed in character, and chiefly because we have accepted low ideals and inferior standards imposed upon us by social elements betrayed and abandoned by a world that could not aid them or assimilate them since itself had betrayed the only thing that could give them force, unity and coherency, that is, a vital and pervasive religious faith.

There are those who hold our case to be desperate, to whom the disillusionment of peace, after the high optimism engendered by the vast heroism and the exalted ideals instigated by the war, has brought nothing but a mood of deep pessimism. The sentiment is perhaps natural, but it is none the less both irrational and wicked. If it is persisted in, if it becomes widespread, it may perfectly well justify itself, but only so. We no longer accept the Calvinistic doctrine of predestination, we believe, and must highly believe, that our fate is of our own making, for Christianity has made us the heirs of free-will. What we will that shall we be, or rather, what we *are* that shall we will, and if we make of ourselves what, by the grace of God, we may, then the victory rests with us. It is true that we are in the last years of a definite period, on that decline that precedes the opening of a new epoch. Never in history has any such period overpassed its limit of five hundred years, and ours, which came to birth in the last half of the fifteenth century, cannot outlast the present. But these declining years are preceding those wherein all things are made new, and the next two generations will see, not alone the passing of what we may call modernism, since it is our own age, but the prologue of the epoch that is to come. It is for us to say what this shall be. It is not foreordained; true, if we will it, it may be a reign of disaster, a parallel to the well-recognized "Dark Ages" of history, but also, if we will, it may be a new and a true "renaissance," a rebirth of old ideals, of old honour, of old faith, only incarnate in new and noble forms.

The vision of an old heaven and a new earth was vouchsafed us during the war, when horror and dishonour and degradation were shot through and through with an epic heroism and chivalry and self-sacrifice. What if this all did fade in the miasma of Versailles and the cynicism of trade fighting to get back to "normalcy," and the red anarchy out of the East? There is no fiat of God that fixes these things as eternal. Even they also may be made the instruments of revelation and re-creation. Paris and London, Rome, Berlin and Washington are meshed in the tangled web of the superannuated who cannot escape the incubus of the old ways and the old theories that were themselves the cause of the war and of the failure of "modern civilization," but another generation is taking the field and we must believe that this has been burned out of them. They may have achieved this great perfection in the field, they may have experienced it through those susceptible years of life just preceding military age. It does not matter. Somehow they have it, and those who come much in contact in school or college with boys and men between the ages of seventeen and twenty-five, know, and thankfully confess, that if they can control the event the future is secure.

In the harlequinade of fabulous material success the nations of "modern civilization" suffered a moral deterioration, in themselves and in their individual members; by a moral regeneration they may be saved. How is this to be accomplished? How, humanly speaking, is the redemption of society to be achieved? Not alone by change of heart in each individual, though if this could be it would be enough. Humanly speaking there is not time and we dare not hope for the divine miracle whereby "in the twinkling of an eye we shall all be changed." Still less by sole reliance on some series of new political, social, economic and educational devices; there is no plan, however wise and profound, that can work effectively under the dead weight of a society that is made up of individuals whose moral sense is defective. Either of these two methods, put into operation by itself, will fail. Acting together they may succeed.

I repeat what I have said before. The material thing and the spiritual force work by inter-action and cooerdinately. The abandonment or reform of some device that has proved evil or inadequate, and the substitution of something better, changes to that extent the environment of the individual and so enables him more perfectly to develop his inherent possibilities in character and capacity, while every advance in this direction reacts on the machinery of life and makes its improvement more possible. With a real sense of my own personal presumption, but with an equally real sense of the responsibility that rests on every man at the present crisis, I shall venture certain suggestions as to possible changes that may well be effected in the material forms of contemporary society as well as in its methods of thought, in order that the spiritual energies of the individual may be raised to a higher level through the amelioration of a hampering environment, and, with even greater diffidence, others that may bear more directly on the character-development of the individual. In following out this line of thought I shall, in the remaining seven lectures, speak successively on: A Working Philosophy; The Social Organism; The Industrial and Economic Problem; The Political Organization of Society; The Function of Education and Art; The Problem of Organic Religion; and Personal Responsibility.

I am only too conscious of the fact that the division of my subject under these categorical heads, and the necessities of special argument, if not indeed of special pleading, have forced me to such particular stress on each subject as may very likely give an impression of undue emphasis. If each lecture were to be taken by itself, such an impression would, I fear, be unescapable; I ask therefore for the courtesy of a suspension of judgment until the series is completed, for it is only when taken as a whole, one paper reacting upon and modifying another, that whatever merit the course possesses can be made apparent.

II
A WORKING PHILOSOPHY[1]

The first reaction of the World War was a great interrogation, and the technical "Peace" that has followed brings only reiteration. Why did these things come, and how? The answers are as manifold as the clamourous tongues that ask, but none carries conviction and the problem is still unsolved. According to all rational probabilities we had no right to expect the war that befell; according to all the human indications as we saw them revealed amongst the Allies we had a right to expect a better peace; according to our abiding and abounding faith we had a right to expect a great bettering of life after the war, and even in spite of the peace. It is all a ***non sequitur,*** and still we ask the reason and the meaning of it all.

It may be very long before the full answer is given, yet if we are searching the way towards "The Great Peace" we must establish some working theory, if only that we may redeem our grave errors and avoid like perils in the future. The explanation I assume for myself, and on which I must work, is that, in spite of our intentions (which were of the best) we were led into the development, acceptance and application of a false philosophy of life which was not only untenable in itself but was vitiated and made noxious through its severance from vital religion. In close alliance with this declension of philosophy upon a basis that had been abandoned by the Christian world for a thousand years, perhaps as the ultimate reason for its occurrence, was the tendency to void religion of its vital power, to cut it out of in-

---
[1] This lecture has been very considerably re-written since it was delivered, and much of the matter it then contained has been cut out, and is now printed in the Appendix. These excisions were purely speculative, and while they have a certain bearing on the arguments and conclusions in the other lectures, might very well be prejudicial to them, and for this reason it has seemed better to remove them from the general sequence and give them a supplementary place by themselves.

timate contact with life, and, in the end, to abandon it altogether as an energizing force interpenetrating all existence and controlling it in certain definite directions and after certain definite methods.

The rather complete failure of our many modern and ingenious institutions, the failure of institutionalism altogether, is due far less to wrong theories underlying them, or to radical defects in their technique, than it is to this false philosophy and this progressive abandonment of religion. The wrong theories were there, and the mechanical defects, for the machines were conditioned by the principle that lay behind them, but effort at correction and betterment will make small progress unless we first regain the right religion and a right philosophy. I said this to Henri Bergson last year in Paris and his reply was significant as coming from a philosopher. "Yes," he said, "you are right; and of the two, the religion is the more important."

If we had this back, and in full measure; if society were infused by it, through and through, and men lived its life, and in its life, philosophy would take care of itself and the nature of our institutions would not matter. On the other hand, without it, no institution can be counted safe, or will prove efficacious, while no philosophy, however lofty and magisterial, can take its place, or even play its own part in the life of man or society. I must in these lectures say much about institutions themselves, but first I shall try to indicate what seem to me the more serious errors in current philosophy, leaving until after a study of the material forms which are so largely conditioned by the philosophical attitude, the consideration of that religion, both organic and personal, which I believe can alone verify the philosophy, give the institutions life and render them reliable agencies for good.

For a working definition of philosophy, in the sense in which I use it here, I will take two sayings, one out of the thirteenth century, one from the twentieth. "They are called wise who put things in their right order and control them well," says St. Thomas Aquinas. "Philosophy is the science of the totality of things," says Cardinal Mercier, his greatest contemporary commentator, and he continues, "Philosophy is the sum-total of reality." Philosophy is the body of **human** wisdom, verified and irradiated by divine wisdom. "The science of the totality of things": not the isolation of individual phenomena, or even of groups of phenomena, as is the method of the natural sciences, but the setting of all in their varied relationships and values, the antithesis of that narrowness and concentration of vision that follow intensive specialization and have issue in infinite delusions and unrealities, "Philosophy regards the sum-total of reality" and it achieves this consciousness of reality, first by establishing right relations between phenomena, and then, abandoning the explicit intellectual process, by falling back on divine illumination which enables it to see through those well-ordered phenomena the Divine Actuality that lies behind, informing them with its own finality and using them both as types and as media of transmission and communication. So men are enabled by philosophy "to put things in their right order" and by religion "to control them well," thus becoming indeed worthy to be "called wise."

Now, from the beginnings of conscious life, man has found himself surrounded and besieged by un-calculable phenomena. Beaten upon by forces he could not estimate or predict or control, he has sought to solve their sphynx-like riddle, to establish some plausible relation between them, to erect a logical scheme of things. Primitive man, as Worringer demonstrates in his "Form Problems of the Gothic," strove to achieve something of certitude and fixity through the crude but definite lines and forms of neolithic art. Classical man brought into play the vigour and subtlety and ingenuity of intellect in its primal and most dynamic form, expressed through static propositions of almost mathematical exactness. The peoples of the East rejected the intellectual-mathematical method and solution and sought a way out through the mysterious operation of the inner sense that manifests itself in the form of emotion. With the revelation of Christianity came also, and of course, enlightenment, which was not definite and closed at some given moment, but progressive and cumulative. At once, speaking philosophically, the intellectual method of the West and the intuitive method of the East came together and fused in a new thing, each element limiting, and at the same time fortifying the other, while the opposed obscurities of the past were irradiated by the revealing and creative spirit of Christ. So came the beginnings of that definitive Christian philosophy which was to proceed from Syria, Anatolia and Constantinople, through Alexandria to St. Augustine, and was to find its fullest expression during the Middle Ages and by means of Duns Scotus, Albertus Magnus, Hugh of St. Victor and St. Thomas Aquinas.

It is an interesting fact, though apart from my present consideration, that this philosophical fusion was paralleled in the same places and at the same time, by an aesthetic fusion that brought into existence the first great and consistent art of

Christianity. This question is admirably dealt with in Lisle March Phillipps' "Form and Colour."

This great Christian philosophy which lay behind all the civilization of the Middle Ages, was positive, comprehensive and new. It demonstrated divine purpose working consciously through all things with a result in perfect coherency; it gave history a new meaning as revealing reality and as a thing forever present and never past, and above all it elucidated the nature of both matter and spirit and made clear their operation through the doctrine of sacramentalism.

In the century that saw the consummation of this great philosophical system--as well as that of the civilization which was its expositor in material form--there came a separation and a divergence. The balanced unity was broken, and on the one hand the tendency was increasingly towards the exaggerated mysticism that had characterized the Eastern moiety of the synthesis, on the other towards an exaggerated intellectualism the seeds of which are inherent even in St. Thomas himself. The new mysticism withdrew further and further from the common life, finding refuge in hidden sanctuaries in Spain, Italy, the Rhineland; the old intellectualism became more and more dominant in the minds of man and the affairs of the world, and with the Renaissance it became supreme, as did the other qualities of paganism in art as well as in every other field of human activity.

The first fruit of the new intellectualism was the philosophy of Dr. John Calvin--if we can call it such,--Augustinian philosophy, misread, distorted and made noxious by its reliance on the intellectual process cut off from spiritual energy as the sufficient corrective of philosophical thought. It is this false philosophy, allied with an equally false theology, that misled for so many centuries those who accepted the new versions of Christianity that issued out of the Reformation. The second was the mechanistic system, or systems, the protagonist of which was Descartes. If, as I believe, Calvinism was un-Christian, the materialistic philosophies that have gone on from the year 1637, were anti-Christian. As the power of Christianity declined through the centuries that have followed the Reformation, Calvinism played a less and less important part, while the new philosophies of mechanism and rationalism correspondingly increased. During the nineteenth century their control was absolute, and what we are today we have become through this dominance, coupled with the general devitalizing or abandonment of religion.

And yet are we not left comfortless. Even in the evolutionary philosophy engendered by Darwin and formulated by Herbert Spencer and the Germans, with all its mistaken assumptions and dubious methods, already there is visible a tendency to get away from the old Pagan static system reborn with the Renaissance. We can never forget that Bergson has avowed that "the mind of man, by its very nature, is incapable of apprehending reality." After this the return towards the scholastic philosophy of the Middle Ages is not so difficult, nor even its recovery. If we associate with this process on the part of formal philosophy the very evident, if sometimes abnormal and exaggerated, progress towards a new mysticism, we are far from finding ourselves abandoned to despair as to the whole future of philosophy.

Now this return and this recovery are, I believe, necessary as one of the first steps towards establishing a sound basis for the building up of a new and a better civilization, and one that is in fact as well as in name a Christian civilization. I do not mean that, with this restoration of Christian philosophy, there we should rest. Both revelation and enlightenment are progressive, and once the nexus of our broken life were restored, philosophical development would be continuous, and we should go on beyond the scholastics even as they proceeded beyond Patristic theology and philosophy. I think a break of continuity was effected in the sixteenth century, with disastrous effects, and until this break is healed we are cut off from what is in a sense the Apostolical succession of philosophical verity.

Before going further I would guard against two possible misconceptions; of one of them I have already spoken, that is, the error so frequent in the past as well as today, that would make of philosophy, however sound, however consonant with the finalities of revealed religion, a substitute in any degree for religion itself. Philosophy is the reaction of the intellect, of man to the stimuli of life, but religion *is* life and is therefore in many ways a flat contradiction of the concepts of the intellect, which is only a small portion of life, therefore limited, partial, and (because of this) sometimes entirely wrong in its conclusions independently arrived at along these necessarily circumscribed lines.

The second possible error is that philosophy is the affair of a small group of students and specialists, quite outside the purview of the great mass of men, and that it owes its existence to this same class of delving scholars, few in number, impractical in their aims, and sharply differentiated from their fellows. On the contrary it is a vital consideration for all those who desire to "see life and see it whole" in order that they may establish a true scale of comparative values and a right relationship between those things that come from the outside and, meeting those that come from within, establish that plexus of interacting force we call life. As for the source of philosophic truth, Friar Bacon put it well when he said "All the wisdom of philosophy is created by God and given to the philosophers, and it is Himself that illumines the minds of men in all wisdom." It is a whimsical juxtaposition, but the first pastor of the Puritans in America, the Rev. John Robinson, testifies to the same effect. "All truth," he says, "is of God ... Wherefore it followeth that nothing true in right reason and sound philosophy can be false in divinity.... I add, though the truth be uttered by the devil himself, yet it is originally of God." There are not two sources of truth, that of Divine Revelation on the one hand, that of science and philosophy and all the intellectual works of man on the other. Truth is one, and the Source is one; the channels of communication alone are different. But truth in its finality, the Absolute, the ***noumenon*** that is the substance of phenomena, is in itself not a thing that can be directly apprehended by man; it lies within the "ultra-violet" rays of his intellectual spectrum. "The trammels of the body prevent man from knowing God in Himself" says Philo, "He is known only in the Divine forces in which He manifests Himself." And St. Thomas: "In the present state of life in which the soul is united to a passable body, it is impossible for the intellect to understand anything actually except by turning to the phantasm." Religion confesses this, philosophy constantly tends to forget it, therefore true religion speaks always through the symbol, rejecting, because it transcends, the intellectual criterion, while philosophy is on safe ground only when it unites itself with religion, testing its own conclusions by a higher reality, and existing not as a rival but as a coadjutor.

It is St. Paul who declares that "God has never left Himself without a witness" and the "witness" was explicit, however clouded, in the philosophies of paganism. Plato and Aristotle knew the limitations of man's mind, and the corrective of overweaning intellectuality in religion, but thereafter the wisdom faded and pride ousted humility, with the result that philosophy became not light but darkness. Let me quote from the great twelfth century philosopher, Hugh of St. Victor, who deserves a better fate than sepulture in the ponderous tomes of Migne:

"There was a certain wisdom that seemed such to them that knew not the true wisdom. The world found it and began to be puffed up, thinking itself great in this. Confiding in its wisdom it became presumptuous and boasted it would attain the highest wisdom. And it made itself a ladder of the face of creation.... Then those things which were seen were known and there were other things which were not known; and through those which were manifest they expected to reach those that were hidden. And they stumbled and fell into the falsehoods of their own imagining.... So God made foolish the wisdom of this world; and He pointed out another wisdom, which seemed foolishness and was not. For it preached Christ crucified, in order that truth might be sought in humility. But the world despised it, wishing to contemplate the works of God, which He had made a source of wonder, and it did not wish to venerate what He had set for imitation, neither did it look to its own disease, seeking medicine in piety; but presuming on a false health, it gave itself over with vain curiosity to the study of alien things."

Precisely: and this is the destiny that has overtaken not only the pagan philosophy of which Hugh of St. Victor was speaking, but also that which followed after St. Thomas Aquinas, from Descartes to Hobbes and Kant and Comte and Herbert Spencer and William James. The jealously intellectual philosophies of the nineteenth century, the materialistic and mechanistic substitutes that were offered and accepted with such enthusiasm after the great cleavage between religion and life, are but "the falsehoods of their own imaginings" of which Hugh of St. Victor speaks, for they were cut off from the stream of spiritual verity, and are losing themselves in the desert they have made.

Meanwhile they have played their part in shaping the destinies of the world, and it was an ill part, if we may judge from the results that showed themselves in the events that have been recorded between the year 1800 and the present moment. Just what this influence was in determining the nature of society, of industrial civilization and of the political organism I shall try to indicate in some of the following lectures, but apart from these concrete happenings, this influence was, I am persuaded, most disastrous in its bearing on human character. Neither wealth nor power, neither education nor environment, not even the inherent tendencies of race--the most powerful of all--can avail against the degenerative force of a life without religion, or, what is worse, that maintains only a desiccated formula; and the post-Renaissance philosophies are one and all definitely anti-religious and self-proclaimed substitutes for religion. As such they were offered and accepted, and as such they must take their share of the responsibility for what has happened.

I believe we must and can retrace our steps to that point in time when a right philosophy was abandoned, and begin again. There is no impossibility or even difficulty here. History is not a dead thing, a thing of the past; it is eternally present to man, and this is one of the sharp differentiations between man and beast. The material monuments of man crumble and disappear, but the spirit that built the Parthenon or Reims Cathedral, that inspired St. Paul on Mars' hill or forged Magna Charta or the Constitution of the United States is, **because of our quality as men,** just as present and operative with us today, if we will, as that which sent the youth of ten nations into a righteous war five years ago, or spoke yesterday through some noble action that you or I may have witnessed. It is as easy for us to accept and practice the philosophy of St. Thomas or the divine humanism of St. Francis as it is to accept the philosophy of Mr. Wells or the theories of Sir Oliver Lodge. No spiritual thing dies, or even grows old, nor does it drift backward in the dwindling perspective of ancient history, and the foolishest saying of man is that "you cannot turn back the hands of the clock."

It is simply a question of will, and will is simply a question of desire and of faith.

Manifestly I cannot be expected to recreate in a few words this philosophy to which I believe we must have recourse in our hour of need. I have no ability to do this in any case. It begins with St. Paul, is continued through St. Augustine, and finds its culmination in the great Mediaeval group of Duns Scotus, Albertus Magnus, Hugh of St. Victor and St. Thomas Aquinas. I do not know of any single book that epitomizes it all in vital form, though Cardinal Mercier and Dr. De Wulf have written much that is stimulating and helpful. I cannot help thinking that the great demand today is for a compact volume that synthesizes the whole magnificent system in terms not of history and scientific exegesis, but in terms of life. Plato and Aristotle are so preserved to man, and the philosophers of modernism also; it is only the magisterial and dynamic philosophy of Christianity that is diffused through many works, some of them still untranslated and all quite without coordination, save St. Thomas Aquinas alone, the magnitude of whose product staggers the human mind and in its profuseness defeats its own ends. We need no more histories of philosophy, but we need an epitome of Christian philosophy, not for students but for men.

Such an epitome I am not fitted to offer, but there are certain rather fundamental conceptions and postulates that run counter both to pagan and to modern philosophy, the loss of which out of life has, I maintain, much to do with our present estate, and that must be regained before we can go forward with any reasonable hope of betterment. These I will try to indicate as well as I can.

Christian philosophy teaches, in so far as it deals with the relationship between man and these divine forces that are forever building, unbuilding and rebuilding the fabric of life, somewhat as follows:

The world as we know it, man, life itself as it works through all creation, is the union of matter and spirit; and matter is not spirit, nor spirit matter, nor is one a mode of the other, but they are two different creatures. Apart from this union of matter and spirit there is no life, in the sense in which we know it, and severance is death. "The body" says St. Thomas, "is not of the essence of the soul; but the soul, by the nature of its essence, can be united to the body, so that, properly speaking, the soul alone is not the species, but the composite", and Duns Scotus makes clear the nature and origin of this common "essence" when he says there is "on the one hand God as Infinite Actuality, on the other spiritual and corporeal substances possessing an homogeneous common element." That is to say; matter and spirit are both the result of the divine creative act, and though separate, and in a sense opposed, find their point of origin in the Divine Actuality.

The created world is the concrete manifestation of matter, through which, for its transformation and redemption, spirit is active in a constant process of interpenetration whereby matter itself is being eternally redeemed. What then is matter and what is spirit? The question is of sufficient magnitude to absorb all the time assigned to these lectures, with the strong possibility that even then we should be scarcely wiser than before. For my own purposes, however, I am content to accept the definition of matter formulated by Duns Scotus, which takes over the earlier definition of Plotinus, purges it of its elements of pagan error, and redeems it by Christian insight.

"Materia Primo Prima" says the great Franciscan, "is the indeterminate element of contingent things. This does not exist in Nature, but it has reality in so far as it constitutes the term of God's creative activity. By its union with a substantial form it becomes endowed with the attributes of quantity, and becomes Secundo Prima. Subject to the substantial changes of Nature, it becomes matter as we see it."

It is this "Materia Primo Prima," the term of God's creative activity, that is eternally subjected to the regenerative process of spiritual interpenetration, and the result is organic life.

What is spirit? The creative power of the Logos, in the sense in which St. John interprets and corrects the early, partial, and therefore erroneous theories of the Stoics and of Philo. God the Son, the Eternal Word of the Father, "the brightness of His glory and the figure of His Substance." "God of God, Light of Light, very God of very God, begotten, not made, being of one substance with the Father: by Whom all things were made." Pure wisdom, pure will, pure energy, unconditioned by matter, but creating life out of the operation of the Holy Spirit on and through matter, and in the fullness of time becoming Incarnate for the purpose of the final redemption of man.

Now since man is so compact of matter and spirit, it must follow that he cannot lay hold of pure spirit, the Absolute that lies beyond and above all material conditioning, except through the medium of matter, through its figures, its symbols, its "phantasms." Says St. Thomas: "From material things we can rise to some kind of knowledge of immaterial things, but not to the perfect knowledge thereof." The way of life therefore, is the incessant endeavour of man sacramentally to approach the Absolute through the leading of the Holy Spirit, so running parallel to the slow perfecting of matter which is being effected by the same operation. So matter itself takes on a certain sanctity, not only as something susceptible, and in process, of perfection, but as the vehicle of spirit and its tabernacle, since in matter spirit is actually incarnate.

From this process follows of necessity the whole sacramental system, in theology, philosophy and operation, of Christianity. It is of its *esse;* its great original, revolutionary and final contribution to the wisdom that man may have for his own, and it follows inevitably from the basic facts of the Incarnation and Redemption, which are also its perfect showing forth.

Philosophically this is the great contribution of Christianity and for fifteen centuries it was held implicitly by Christendom, yet it was rejected, either wholly or in part, by the Protestant organizations that came out of the Reformation, and it fell into such oblivion that outside the Catholic Church it was not so much ignored or rejected as totally forgotten. Recently a series of lectures were delivered at King's College, London, by various carefully chosen authorities, all specialists in their own fields, under the general title "Mediaeval Contributions to Modern Civilization," and neither the pious author of the address on "The Religious Contribution of the Middle Ages," nor the learned author of that on "Mediaeval Philosophy," gave evidence of ever having heard of sacramental philosophy. It may be that I do them an injustice, and that they would offer as excuse the incontestible fact that Mediaevalism contributed nothing to "modern civilization," either in religion or philosophy, that it was willing to accept.

The peril of all philosophies, outside that of Christianity as it was developed under the Catholic dispensation, is dualism, and many have fallen into this grave error. Now dualism is not only the reversal of truth, it is also the destroyer of righteousness.

Sacramentalism is the anthithesis of dualism. The sanctity of matter as the potential of spirit and its dwelling-place on earth; the humanizing of spirit through its condescension to man through the making of his body and all created things its earthly tabernacle, give, when carried out into logical development, a meaning to life, a glory to the world, an elucidation of otherwise unsolvable mysteries, and an impulse toward noble living no other system can afford. It is a real philosophy of life, a standard of values, a criterion of all possible postulates, and as its loss meant the world's peril, so its recovery may mean its salvation.

Now as the philosophy of Christianity is purely and essentially sacramental, so must be the operation of God through the Church. This "Body of Christ" on earth is indeed a fellowship, a veritable communion of the faithful, whether living or dead, but it is also a divine organism which lives, and in which each member lives, not by the preaching of the Word, not even by and through the fellowship in living and worship, but through the ordained channels of grace known as the Sacraments. In accordance with the sacramental system, every material thing is proclaimed as possessing in varying degree sacramental potentiality, while seven great Sacraments were instituted to be, each after its own fashion, a special channel for the inflowing of the power of the Divine Actuality. Each is a symbol, just as so many other created things are, or may become, symbols, but they are also ***realities,*** veritable media for the veritable communications of veritable divine grace. Here is the best definition I know, that of Hugh of St. Victor. "A sacrament is the corporeal or material element set out sensibly, representing from its similitude, signifying from its institution, and containing from its sanctification, some invisible and spiritual grace." This is the unvarying and invariable doctrine of historic Christianity, and the reason for the existence of the Church as a living and functioning organism. The whole sacramental system is in a sense an extension, in time, of the Redemption, just as one particular Sacrament, the Holy Eucharist, is also in a sense an extension of the Incarnation, as it is also an extension, in time, of the Atonement, the Sacrifice of Calvary.

The Incarnation and the Redemption are not accomplished facts, completed nineteen centuries ago; they are processes that still continue, and their term is fixed only by the total regeneration and perfecting of matter, while the Seven Sacraments are the chiefest amongst an infinity of sacramental processes which are the agencies of this eternal transfiguration.

God the Son became Incarnate, not only to accomplish the redemption of men as yet unborn, for endless ages, through the Sacrifice of Calvary, but also to initiate and forever maintain a new method whereby this result was to be more perfectly attained; that is to say, the Church, working through the specific sacramental agencies He had ordained, or was from time to time to ordain, through His everlasting presence in the Church He had brought into being at Pentecost. He did not come to establish in material form a Kingdom of Heaven on Earth, or to provide for its ultimate coming. He indeed established a Spiritual Kingdom, His Church, "in the world, not of it," which is a very different matter indeed, as the centuries have proved. His Kingdom is not of this world, nor will it be established here. There has been no ***absolute*** advance in human development since the Incarnation. Nations rise and fall, epochs wax and wane, civilizations grow out of savagery, crest and sink back into savagery and oblivion. Redemption is for the individual, not for the race, nor yet for society as a whole. Then, and only then, and under that form, it is sure, however long may be the period of its accomplishment. "Time is the ratio of the resistance of matter to the interpenetration of spirit," and by this resistance is the duration of time determined. When it shall have been wholly overcome then "time shall be no more."

See therefore how perfect is the correspondence between the Sacraments and the method of life where they are the agents, and which they symbolically set forth. There is in each case the material form and the spiritual substance, or energy. Water, chrism, oil, the spoken word, the touch of hands, the sign of the cross, and finally and supremely the bread and wine of the Holy Eucharist. Each a material thing, but each representing, signifying and containing some gift of the Holy Spirit, real, absolute and potent. So matter and spirit are linked together in every operation of the Church, from the cradle to the grave, and man has ever before him the eternal revelation of this linked union of matter and spirit in his life, the eternal teaching of the honour of the material thing through its agency and through its existence as the subject for redemption. So also, through the material association, and the divine condescension to his earthly and fallible estate (limited by association with matter only to inadequate presentation) he makes the Spirit of God his own, to dwell therewith after the fashion of man.

And how much this explains and justifies: Man approaches, and must always approach, spiritual things not only through material forms but by means of material agencies. The highest and most beautiful things, those where the spirit seems to achieve its loftiest reaches, are frequently associated with the grossest and most unspiritual forms, yet the very splendour of the spiritual verity redeems and glorifies the material agency, while on the other hand the homeliness, and even animal quality, of the material thing, brings to man, with a poignancy and an appeal that are incalculable, the spiritual thing that, in its absolute essence, would be so far beyond his ken and his experience and his powers of assimilation that it would be inoperative.

This is the true Humanism; not the fictitious and hollow thing that was the offspring of neo-paganism and took to itself a title to which it had no claim. Held tacitly or consciously by the men of the Middle Ages, from the immortal philosopher to the immortal but nameless craftsman, it was the force that built up the noble social structure of the time and poised man himself in a sure equilibrium. Already it had of necessity developed the whole scheme of religious ceremonial and given art a new content and direction through its new service. By analogy and association all material things that could be so used were employed as figures and symbols, as well as agencies, through the Sacraments, and after a fashion that struck home to the soul through the organs of sense. Music, vestments, incense, flowers, poetry, dramatic action, were linked with the major arts of architecture, painting and sculpture, and all became not only ministers to the emotional faculties but direct appeals to the intellect through their function as poignant symbols. So art received its soul, and was almost a living creature until matter and spirit were again divorced in the death that severed them during the Reformation. Thereafter religion had entered upon a period of slow desiccation and sterilization wherever the symbol was cast away with the Sacraments and the faith and the philosophy that had made it live. The bitter hostility to the art and the liturgies and the ceremonial of the Catholic faith is due far less to ignorance of the meaning and function of art and to an inherited jealousy of its quality and its power, than it is to the conscious and determined rejection of the essential philosophy of Christianity, which is sacramentalism.

The whole system was of an almost sublime perfection and simplicity, and the formal Sacraments were both its goal and its type. If they had been of the same value and identical in nature they would have failed of perfect exposition, in the sense in which they were types and symbols. They were not this, for while six of the explicit seven were substantially of one mode, there was one where the conditions that held elsewhere were transcended, and where, in addition to the two functions it was instituted to perform it gave, through its similitude, the clear revelation of the most significant and poignant fact in the vast mystery of life. I mean, of course, the Holy Eucharist, commonly called the Mass.

If matter is *per se* forever inert, unchangeable, indestructible, then we fall into the dilemma of a materialistic monism on the one hand, Manichaean dualism on the other. Even under the most spiritual interpretation we could offer--that, shall we say, of those today who try to run with the hare of religion and hunt with the hounds of rationalistic materialism--matter and spirit unite in man as body and soul, and in the Sacraments as the vehicle and the essence, but temporally and temporarily; doomed always to ultimate severance by death in the one case, by the completion of the sacramental process in the other. If, on the other hand, the object of the universe and of time is the constant redemption and transformation of matter through its interpenetration by spirit in the power of God the Holy Ghost, then we escape the falsities of dualism, while in the miracle of the Mass we find the type and the showing forth of the constant process of life whereby every instant, matter itself is being changed and glorified and transferred from the plane of matter to the plane of spirit.

If this is so: if the Incarnation and the Redemption are not only fundamental facts but also types and symbols of the divine process forever going on here on earth, then, while the other Sacraments are in themselves not only instruments of grace but manifestations of that process whereby in all things matter is used as the vehicle of spirit, the Mass, transcending them all, is not only Communion, not only a Sacrifice acceptable before God, it is also the unique symbol of the redemption and transformation of matter; since, of all the Sacraments, it is the only one where the very physical qualities of the material vehicle are transformed, and while the accidents alone remain, the substance, finite and perishable, becomes, in an instant of time and by the operation of God, infinite and immortal.

It is to sacramentalism then that we must return, not only in religion and its practice, but in philosophy, if we are to establish a firm foundation for that newer society and civilization that are to help us to achieve the "Great Peace." Antecedent systems failed, and subsequent systems have failed; in this alone, the philosophy of Christianity, is there safety, for it alone is consonant with the revealed will of God.

III
THE SOCIAL ORGANISM

Society, that is to say, the association in life of men, women and children, is the fundamental fact of life, and this is so whether the association is of the family, the school, the community, industry or government. Everything else is simply a series of forms, arrangements and devices by which society works, either for good or ill. Man makes or mars himself in and through society. He is responsible for his own soul, but if he sees only this and works directly for his soul's salvation, disregarding the society of which he is a part, he may lose it, whereas, if he is faithful to society and honourably plays his part as a social animal with a soul, he will very probably save it, even though he may for the time have quite ignored its existence. Man is a member of a family, a pupil under education, a worker and a citizen. In all these relationships he is a part of a social group; he is also a component part of the human race and linked in some measure to every other member thereof whether living or dead. Into every organization or institution in which he is involved during his lifetime--family, school, art or craft, trade union, state, church--enters the social equation. If society is ill organized either in theory or in practice, in any or all of its manifestations, then the engines or devices by which it operates will be impotent for good. Defective society cannot produce either a good fundamental law, a good philosophy, a good art, or any other thing. Conversely, these, when brought forth under an wholesome society, will decay and perish when society degenerates.

In its large estate, that is, comprehending all the minor groups, as a nation, a people or an era, society is always in a state of unstable equilibrium, tending either toward better or worse. It may indeed be of the very essence of human life, but it is a plant of tender growth and needs delicate nurture and jealous care; a small thing may work it irreparable injury. It may reach very great heights of perfection and spread over a continent, as during the European Middle Ages; it may sink to low depths with an equal dominion, as in the second dark ages of the nineteenth century. Sometimes little enclaves of high value hide themselves in the midst of degradation, as Venice and Ireland in the Dark Ages. Always, by the grace of God, the primary social unit, the family may, and frequently does, achieve and maintain both purity and beauty when the world without riots in ruin and profligacy.

I have taken the problem of the organization of society as the first to be considered, for it is fundamental. If society is of the wrong shape it does not matter in the least how intelligent and admirable may be the devices we construct for the operation of government or industry or education; they may be masterly products of human intelligence but they will not work, whereas on the other hand a sane, wholesome and decent society can so interpret and administer clumsy and defective instruments that they will function to admiration. A perfect society would need no such engines at all, but a perfect society implies perfect individuals, and I think we are now persuaded that a society of this nature is a purely academic proposition both now and in the calculable future. What we have to do is to take mankind as it is; made up of infinitely varied personalities ranging from the idiot to the "super-man"; cruel and compassionate, covetous and self-sacrificing, silly and erudite, cynical and emotional, vulgar and cultured, brutal and fastidious, shameful in their degradation and splendid in their honour and chivalry, and by the franchise of liberty and the binding of law, facilitate in every way the process whereby they themselves work out their own salvation. You cannot impose morality by statute or guarantee either character or intelligence by the perfection of the machine. Every institution, good or bad, is the result of growth from many human impulses, not the creation of autocratic fiat. But growth may be impeded, hastened, or suspended, and the most that can be done is to offer incentives to action, remove the obstacles to development, and establish conditions and influences that make more easy the finding of the right way.

Now it seems to me that the two greatest obstacles to the development of a right society have been first, the enormous scale in which everything of late has been cast, and second, that element in modern democracy which denies essential differences in human character, capacity and potential, and so logically prohibits social distinctions, and refuses them formal sanction or their recognition through conferred honours. In questioning the validity and the value of these two factors, imperialism and social democracy, and in suggesting substitutes, I am, I suppose, attacking precisely the two institutions which are today--or at all events have been until very recently--held in most conspicuous honour by the majority of people, but the question is at least debateable, and for my own part I have no alternative but to assert their mistaken nature, and to offer the best I can in the way of substitutes.

The question of imperialism, of a gross and unhuman and therefore absolutely wrong scale, is one that will enter into almost all of the matters with which I propose to deal, certainly with industrialism, with politics, with education, with religion, as well as with the immediate problem of the social organism, for not only has it destroyed the human scale in human life, and therefore brought it into the danger of immediate destruction, but it has also been a factor in establishing the quantitative standard in all things, in place of the qualitative standard, and this, in itself, is simply the antecedent of well-merited catastrophe. In considering the social organism, therefore, we must have in mind that this is intimately affected by every organic institution which man has developed and into which he enters in common with others of his kind.

The situation as it confronts us today is one in which man by his very energy and the stimulus of those cosmic energies he has so astonishingly mastered, has got far beyond his depth. I say man has mastered these energies; yes, but this was true only of a brief period in the immediate past. They now have mastered him. It is the old story of the Frankenstein monster over again. Man is not omnipotent, he is not God. There are limits beyond which he cannot go without coming in peril of death. An isolated individual here and there may become super-man, perhaps, though at grievous peril to his own soul, and it is conceivable that to such an one it might be possible to live beyond the human scale, though hardly. If one could envisage so awful a thing as a community made up entirely of super-men, one might concede that here also the human scale might be exceeded without danger of catastrophe. With society as it is, and always will be, a welter of defectives and geniuses in small numbers and a vast majority of just plain men, with all that that implies, the breaking through into the imperial scale is simply a letting in the jungle; walls and palings and stockades, the delicate fabrics of architecture, the clever institutions of law, the thin red line of the army, all melt, crumble, are overcome by the onrush of primordial things, and where once was the white man's city is now the eternal jungle, and the vines and thrusting roots and rank herbage blot out the very memory of a futile civilization, while the monkey and the jackal and the python come again into their heritage.

Alexander and Caesar, Charles V and Louis XIV and Napoleon and Disraeli and William III could function for a few brief years beyond the limits of the human scale, though even they had an end, but you cannot link imperialism and democracy without the certainty of an earlier and a more ignominious fall.

I have already spoken of the malignant and pathological quality of the quantitative standard. It is indeed not only the nemesis of culture but even of civilization itself. Out of this same gross scale of things come many other evils; great states subsisting on the subjugation and exploitation of small and alien peoples; great cities which when they exceed more than 100,000 in population are a menace, when they exceed 1,000,000 are a crime; division of labour and specialization which degrade men to the level of machines; concentration and segregation of industries, the factory system, high finance and international finance, capitalism, trades-unionism and the International, standardized education, "metropolitan" newspapers, pragmatic philosophy, and churches "run on business methods" and recruited by advertising and "publicity agents."

Greater than all, however, is the social poison that effects society with pernicious anaemia through cutting man off from his natural social group and making of him an undistinguishable particle in a sliding stream of grain. Man belongs to his family, his neighbourhood, his local trade or craft guild and to his parish church: the essence of wholesome association is that a man should work with, through and by those whom he knows personally--and preferably so well that he calls them all by their first names.

As a matter of fact, today he works with, through and by the individuals whom he probably has never seen, and frequently would, as a matter of personal taste, hesitate to recognize if he did see them. He belongs to the "local" of a union which is a part of a labour organization which covers the entire United States and is controlled in all essential matters from a point from one hundred to two thousand miles away. He votes for mayor with a group of men, less than one per cent of whom he knows personally (unless he is a professional politician), with another group for state officers, and with the whole voting population of the United States, for President. If he goes to church in a city he finds himself amongst people drawn from every ward and outlying district, if he mixes in "society" he associates with those from everywhere, perhaps, except his own neighbourhood. Only when he is in college, in his club or in his secret society lodge or the quarters of his ward boss does he find himself in intimate social relations with human beings of like mind and a similar social status. He is a cog in a wheel, a thing, a point of potential, a lonely and numerical unit, instead of a gregarious human animal rejoicing in his friends and companions, and working, playing and quarreling with them, as God made him and meant him to be and to do.

Of course the result of this is that men are forced into unnatural associations, many of which are purely artificial and all of which are unsound. It is true that the trade union, the professional society, the club are natural and wholesome expressions of common and intimate interests, but they acquire a false value when they are not balanced and regulated by a prior and more compelling association which cuts, not vertically but horizontally through society, that is to say, the neighbourhood or community group. The harsh and perilous division into classes and castes which is now universal, with its development of "class consciousness," is the direct and inevitable result of this imperial scale in life which has annihilated the social unit of human scale and brought in the gigantic aggregations of peoples, money, manufacture and labourers, where man can no longer function either as a human unit or an essential factor in a workable society.

It is hard to see just how we are to re-fashion this impossible society in terms even nearly approaching the normal and the human. It is universal, and it is accepted by everyone as very splendid and quite the greatest achievement of man. It is practically impossible for any one today to conceive of a world where great empires, populous cities, mills and factories and iron-works in their thousands, and employing their millions through their billions of capitalization, where the stock exchange and the great banking houses and the insurance companies and the department stores, the nation-wide trade unions and professional associations and educational foundations and religious corporations, do not play their predominant part. Nevertheless they are an aggregation of false values, their influence is anti-social, and their inherent weakness was so obviously revealed through the War and the Peace that it has generally escaped notice.

There seem but two ways in which the true scale of life can be restored; either these institutions will continue, growing greater and more unwieldy with increasing speed until they burst in anarchy and chaos, and after ruin and long rest we begin all over again (as once before after the bursting of Roman imperialism), or we shall repeat history (as we always do) only after another fashion and, learning as we always can from the annals of monasticism, build our small communities of the right shape and scale in the very midst of the imperial states themselves, so becoming perhaps the leavening of the lump. This of course is what the monasteries of St. Benedict did in the sixth century and those of the Cluniacs and the Cistercians in the eleventh, and it is what the Franciscans and Dominicans tried to do in the fourteenth century, and failed because the fall of the cultural and historic wave had already begun.

The trouble today with nearly all schemes of reform and regeneration is that they are infected with the very imperialism in scale that has produced the conditions they would redeem. Socialism is now as completely materialistic as the old capitalism, and as international in its scope and methods. Anarchy is becoming imperial and magnificent in its operations. Secular reformers must organize vast committees with intricate ramifications and elaborate systems supported by "drives" for money which must run into at least seven figures, and by vast and efficient bureaus for propaganda, before they can begin operations, and then the chief reliance for success is frequently placed on legislation enacted by the highest lawmaking bodies in the land. Even religion has now surrendered to the same obsession of magnitude and efficiency, and nothing goes (or tries to, it doesn't always succeed) unless it is conceived in gigantic "nation-wide" terms and is "put across" by efficiency experts, highly paid organizers, elaborate "teams" of propagandists and solicitors, and plenty of impressive advertising. A good deal can be bought this way, but it will not "stay bought," for no reform of any sort can be established after any such fashion, since reform begins in and with the individual, and if it succeeds at all it will be by the cumulative process.

I shall speak of this element of scale in every succeeding lecture, for it vitiates every institution we have. Here, where I am dealing with society in itself, I can only say that I believe the sane and wholesome society of the future will eliminate great cities and great corporations of every sort. It will reverse the whole system of specialization and the segregation and unification of industries and the division of labour. It will build upward from the primary unit of the family, through the neighbourhood, to the small, and closely knit, and self-supporting community, and so to the state and the final unifying force which links together a federation of states. In general it will be a return in principle, though not in form, to the social organization of a Mediaeval Europe before the extinction of feudalism on the Continent, and the suppression of the monasteries and the enclosure of the common lands in England.

The grave perils of this false scale in human society have been recognized by many individuals ever since the thing itself became operative, and every Utopia conceived by man during the last two centuries, whether it was theoretical or actually put into ephemeral practice, has been couched in terms of revolt away from imperialism and towards the unit of human scale. In every case however, the introduction of some form of communism has been the ruin of those projects actually materialized, for this in itself is imperialistic in its nature. Communism implies the standard of the gross aggregate, the denial of human differentiation and the quantitative standard, as well as the elimination of private property and the negation of sacred individuality. Its institution implies an almost immediate descent into anarchy with a sequent dictatorship and autocracy, for it is the reversal of the foundation laws of life. Such reversals cannot last, nothing can last that is inimical to flourishing life; it may triumph for a day but life itself sloughs it off as a sound body rids itself of some foreign substance through the sore that festers, bursts and, the septic conditions done away with, heals itself and returns to normal.

Now the inhuman scale has produced one set of septic conditions in society while what is commonly called "democratization" has produced another. We have a bloated society, but also we have one in which a false theory has grown up and been put in practice, in accordance with which an uniformity of human kind has been assumed which never has existed and does not now, and in the effort to enforce this false theory the achievement of distinction has been impeded, leadership discouraged and leaders largely eliminated, the process of leveling downward carried to a very dangerous point, the sane and vital organization of society brought near to an end and a peculiarly vicious scale and standard of social values established. I have urged the return to human scale in human associations, but this does not imply any admixture of communism, which is its very antithesis, still less does it permit the retention of the theoretical uniformity and the unescapable leveling process of so-called democracy.

Before the law all men are equal, that is, they are entitled to even-handed justice. Before God all men are equal, that is, they are granted charity and mercy which transcends the law, also they possess immortal souls of equal value. Here their equality stops. In every other respect they vary in character, capacity, intelligence and potentiality for development along any or all these lines, almost beyond the limits of computation. A sane society will recognize this, it will organize itself accordingly, it will deny to one what it will concede to another, it will foster emulation and reward accomplishment, and it will add another category to those in which all men are equal, that is, the freest scope for advancement, and the greatest facility for passing from one social group into another, the sole test being demonstrated merit.

I am prepared at this point to use the word "aristocracy" for we have the thing even now, only in its worst possible form. The word itself means two things: a government by the best and most able citizens and, to quote a standard dictionary "Persons noted for superiority in any character or quality, taken collectively." There is no harm here, but the harm comes, and the odium also, and justly, when an aristocratic government degenerates into an oligarchy of privilege without responsibility, and when socially it is not "superiority in character or quality" but political cunning, opulence and sycophancy that are the touchstones to recognition and acceptance. The latter are the antithesis of Christianity and common sense, the former is consonant with both and, paradoxical as it may seem, it is also the fulfilling of the ideals of a real democracy, since its honours and distinctions imply service, its relations with those in other estates are reciprocal, it is not a closed caste but the prize of meritorious achievement, and it is therefore equality of opportunity, utilization of ability and the abolition of privilege without responsibility.

Men are forever and gloriously struggling onward towards better things, but there is always the gravitational pull of original sin which scientists denominate "reversion to type." The saving grace in the individual is the divine gift of faith, hope and charity implanted in every soul. These every man must guard and cherish for they are the way of advancement in character. But society is man in association with men, in a sense a new and complex personality, and the same qualities are as necessary here as in the individual. Society, like man, may be said to possess body, soul and spirit, and it must function vitally along all these lines if it is to maintain a normal and wholesome existence. Somewhere there must be something that achieves high ideals of honour, chivalry, courtesy; that maintains right standards of comparative value, and that guards the social organism as a whole from the danger of surrender to false and debased standards, to plausible demagogues, and to mob-psychology.

The greater the prevalence of democratic methods, the greater is the danger of this surrender to propaganda of a thousand sorts and to the dominance of the demagogue, and the existence of an estate fortified by the inheritance of high tradition, measurably free from the necessity of engaging too strenuously in the "struggle for life," guaranteed security of status so long as it does not betray the ideals of its order, but open to accessions from other estates on the basis of conspicuous merit alone, such a force operating in society has proved, and will prove, the best guardian of civilization as a whole and of the interests and liberties of those who may rank in what are known as lower social scales.

But, it may be objected, such an institution as this has never existed. Every political or social aristocracy in history has been mixed and adulterated with bad characters and recreant representatives. There never has been and never will be a perfect aristocracy. Quite true; neither has there ever been a perfect democracy, or a perfect monarchy for that matter. As men we work with imperfections, but we live by faith, and our sole duty is to establish the highest ideals, and to compass them, in so far as we may, with unfailing courage, patience and steadfastness. The ***ideal*** of democracy is a great ideal, but the ***working*** of democracy has been a failure because, amongst other things, it has tried to carry on without the aid of true aristocracy. If the two can be united, first in ideal and in theory, then in operation, our present failure may be changed into victory.

What, after all, does this imply, so far as the social organism is concerned? It seems to me, something like this. First of all, recognition of the fact that there are differences in individuals, in strains of blood, in races, that cannot be overcome by any power of education and environment, and can only be changed through very long periods of time, and that these differences must work corresponding differences in position, function and status in the social organism. Second, that since society automatically develops an aristocracy of some sort or other, and apparently cannot be stopped from doing this, it must be protected from the sort of thing it has produced of late, which is based on money, political expediency and the unscrupulous cleverness of the demagogue, and given a more rational substitute in the shape of a permanent group representing high character and the traditions of honour, chivalry and courtesy. Third, that character and service should be fostered and rewarded by that formal and august recognition, that secure and unquestioned status, and those added opportunities for service that will form a real and significant distinction. Finally, that this order or estate must be able to purge itself of unworthy material, and also must be freely open to constant accessions from without, whatever the source, and for proved character and service.

I fear I must argue this case of the inequality in individual potential, that inequality that does not yield to complex education or favourable environment, for it is fundamental. If it does not exist, then my argument for the organization of society along lines that recognize and regularize diversity of social status and functions, falls to the ground. I affirm that, the doctrine of evolution and modern democratic theory to the contrary, it does exist and that the mitigating influence of education, environment and inherited acquired characters, is small at best.

Let us take the most obvious concrete examples. There are certain ethnic units or races which for periods ranging from five hundred to two thousand years have produced ***character***, and through character the great contributions that have been made to human culture and have been expressed through men of distinction, dynamic force, and vivid personality. Such, amongst many, are the Greeks, the Jews, the Romans, the Normans, the Franks, the "Anglo-Saxons," and the Celts. There are others that in all history have produced nothing. There are certain family names which are a guarantee of distinction, dynamic force, and vivid personality. There are thousands of these names, and they are to be found amongst all the races that have contributed towards the development of culture and civilization. On the other hand, there are far more that have produced nothing distinctive, and possibly never will.

What is the reason for this? Is it the result of blind chance, of accidents that have left certain races and families isolated in stagnant eddies from which some sudden current of a whimsical tide might sweep them out into the full flood of progress, until they then overtook and passed their hitherto successful rivals, who, in their turn, would drift off into progressive incompetence and degeneracy? Biology does not look with enthusiasm on the methods of chance and accident. The choice and transmission of the forty-eight chromosomes that give to each individual his character-potential are probably in accordance with some obscure biological law through which the unfathomable divine will operates. Now these chromosomes may be selected and combined after a fashion, and with a persistence of continuity, that would guarantee character-potential, for good or for ill, through many generations, or they might be so varied in their combinations that no distinct traits would be carried over from one generation to another. As a matter of experience all these three processes take place and are recorded in families of distinct quality, good, bad and indifferent. If the character-potential is predetermined, then manifestly education and environment can play only the subordinate part of fostering its development or retarding it.

In the same way the character and career of the various races of men are determined by the potential inherent in the individuals and families that compose them, and like them the races themselves are for long periods marked by power and capacity or weakness and lack of distinction. There are certain races, such as the Hottentot, the Malay, the American Indian, and mixed bloods, as the Mexican peons and Mongol-Slavs of a portion of the southeastern Europe, that, so far as recorded history is concerned, are either static or retrogressive. There are family units, poverty-stricken and incompetent, in Naples, Canton, East Side New York; or opulent and aggressive in West Side New York, in Birmingham, Westphalia, Pittsburgh, that are no more subject to the cultural and character-creating influences of education and environment--beyond a certain definite point--than are the amphibians of Africa or the rampant weeds of my garden.

This is a hard saying and a provocative. The entire course of democratic theory, of humanitarian thought and of the popular type of scientific speculation stands against it, and the Christian religion as well, unless the statement itself is guarded by exact definitions. If the contention of the scientific materialist were correct, and the thing that makes man, and that Christians call the immortal soul, were but the result of physical processes of growth and differentiation, then slavery would be justifiable, and exploitation a reasonable and inevitable process. Since, however, this assumption of materialism is untenable, and since all men are possessed of immortal souls between which is no distinction in the sight of God, the situation, regrettable if you like, is one which at the same time calls for the exercise of a higher humanitarianism than that so popular during the last generation, and as well for a very drastic revision of contemporary political and social and educational methods.

The soul of the man is the localization of divinity; in a sense each man is a manifestation of the Incarnation. Black or white, conspicuous or obscure, intelligent or stupid, offspring of a creative race or bound by the limitations of one that is static or in process of decay, there is no difference in the universal claim to justice, charity, and opportunity. The soul of a Cantonese river-man, of a Congo slave, of an East Side Jew, is in itself as essentially precious and worth saving as the soul of a bishop, of a descendant of a Norman viking or an Irish king, or that of a volunteer soldier in the late armies of France or Great Britain or the United States.

Here lies absolute and final equality, and the State, the Law, the Church are bound to guard this equality in the one case and the other with equal force; indeed, those of the lower racial and family types claim even more faithful guardianship than those of the higher, for they can accomplish less for themselves and by themselves. But the fundamental and inescapable inequality, in intellect, in character, and in capacity, which I insist is one of the conditioning factors in life, is vociferously denied, but ruthlessly enforced, by the people that will be the first to denounce any restatement of what is after all no more than a patent fact.

A little less enthusiasm for shibboleths, and a little more intelligent regard for history and palpable conditions, will show that the assumed equality between men "on the strength of their manhood alone," the sufficiency of education for correcting the accidental differences that show themselves, and the scheme of life that is worked out along democratic lines on the basis of this essential (or potential) equality, are "fond things vainly imagined" which must be radically modified before the world can begin a sane and wholesome building-up after the great purgation of war.

That equality between men which exists by virtue of the presence in each of an immortal soul, involves an even distribution of justice and the protection of law, without distinction of persons, and an even measure of charity and compassion, but it does not involve the admission of a claim to equality of action or the denial of varied status, since race-values, both of blood and of the ***gens*** enter in to establish differences in character, in intelligence and in capacity which cannot be changed by education, environment or heredity within periods which are practical considerations with society. If we could still hold the old Darwinian dogmas of the origin of species through the struggle for existence and the survival of the fittest, and if the equally august and authoritative dogma of the transmission by inheritance of acquired characteristics were longer tenable, then perhaps we might invoke faith, hope and patience and continue our generous method of imperilling present society while we fixed our eyes on the vision of that to come when environment, education and heredity had accomplished their perfect work. Unfortunately--or perhaps fortunately--science is rapidly reconsidering its earlier and somewhat hasty conclusions, and the consensus of the most authoritative opinion seems to be that we must believe these things no longer. Failing these premises, on which we have laboured so long and so honestly and so sincerely, we are again thrown back on the testimony of history and our own observation, and with this reversal we also are bound to reconsider both our premises and the constitution of those systems and institutions we have erected on them as a foundation.

The existence of a general law does not exclude exceptions. The fact that in the case of human beings we have to take into consideration a powerful factor that does not come into play in the domain of zooelogy and botany--the immortal soul--makes impossible the drawing of exact deductions from precedents therein established. This determining touch of the divine, which is no result of biological processes, but stands outside the limitations of heredity and environment and education, may manifest itself quite as well in one class as in another, for "God is no respecter of persons." As has been said before, there is no difference in degree as between immortal souls. The point is, however, that each is linked to a specific congeries of tendencies, limitations, effective or defective agencies, that are what they have been made by the parents of the race. These may be such as enable the soul to triumph in its earthly experience and in its bodily housing; they may be such as will bring about failure and defeat. It is not that the soul builds itself "more stately mansions"; it is that these are provided for it by the physical processes of life, and it is almost the first duty of man to see that they are well built.

Again, the soul is single and personal; as it is not a plexus of inherited tendencies, so it is not heritable, and a great soul showing suddenly in the dusk of a dull race contributes nothing of its essential quality to the issue of the body it has made its house. The stews of a mill town may suddenly be illuminated by the radiance of a divine soul, to the amazement of profligate parents and the confusion of eugenists; but unless the unsolvable mystery of life has determined on a new species, and so by a sudden influx of the ***elan vital*** cuts off the line of physical succession and establishes one that is wholly new, then the brightness dies away with the passing of the splendid soul, and the established tendencies resume their sway.

The bearing of this theory on the actions of society is immediate. Through the complete disregard of race-values that has obtained during the last two or three centuries, and the emergence and complete supremacy in all categories of life of human groups of low potential, civilization has been brought down to a level where it is threatened with disaster. If recovery is to be effected and a second era of "dark ages" avoided, there must be an entirely new evaluation of things, a new estimate of the principles and methods that obtained under Modernism, and a fearless adventure into fields that may prove not to be so unfamiliar as might at first appear.

Specifically, we must revise our attitude as to immigration, excluding whole classes, and even races, that we have hitherto welcomed with open hands from the disinterested offices of steamship companies: we must control and in some cases prohibit, the mating of various racial stocks; finally we must altogether disallow the practice of changing, by law, one race-name for another. This process is one for which no excuse exists and unless it can be brought to an end then, apart from certain physical differentiations on which nature wisely insists, we have no guaranty against the adulteration that has gone so far towards substituting the mongrel for the pure racial type, while society is bound to suffer still further deception and continued danger along the lines that have recently been indicated by the transformation of Treibitsch into "Lincoln," Braunstein into "Trotsky" and Samuels into "Montague."

For its fulfillment, then, and its regeneration, the real democracy demands and must achieve the creation and cooperation of a real aristocracy, not an aristocracy of material force either military or civil, nor one of land owners or money-getters, nor one of artificial caste. All these substitutes have been tried from time to time, in Rome, China, Great Britain, the United States, and all have failed in the end, for all have ignored the one essential point of ***character***, without which we shall continue to reproduce what we have at present; a thing as insolent, offensive and tyrannical as the old aristocracies at their worst, with none of the constructive and beneficent qualities of the old aristocracies at their best.

That race-values have much to do with this development of character I believe to be true, but of far greater efficiency, indeed the actual motive force, is the Christian religion, working directly on and through the individual and using race as only one of its material means of operation. Democracy has accomplished its present failure, not only because it could not function without the cooperation of aristocracy, but chiefly because, in its modernist form, it has become in fact isolated from Christianity. All in it of good it derives from that Catholic Christianity of the Middle Ages which first put it into practice, all in it of evil it owes to a falling back on paganism and a denial of its own parentage and rejection of its control. I shall deal with this later in more detail; I speak of it now just for the purpose of entering a caveat against any deduction from what I have said that any natural force, of race or evolution or anything else, or any formal institution devised by man, ever has, or ever can, serve in itself as a way of social redemption. I am anxious not to overemphasize these things on which the development of my argument forces me to lay particular stress.

For those who can go with me so far, the question will arise: How then are we so to reorganize society that we may gain the end in view? It is a question not easy of solution. Granted the fact of social differentiation and the necessity of its recognition, how are we to break down the wholly wrong system that now obtains and substitute another in its place? It would be simple enough if within the period allowed us by safety (apparently not any too extended at the present moment) a working majority of men could achieve, in the old and exact phraseology, that change of heart, that spiritual conversion, that would bring back into permanent authority the supernatural virtues of faith, hope, and charity, and that sense of right values in life, which together make almost indifferent the nature of the formal devices man creates for the organization of society. Certainly this is possible; greater miracles have happened in history but, failing this, what?

One turns of course by instinct to old models, but in this is the danger of an attempt at an archaeological restoration, a futile effort at reviving dead forms that have had their day. In principle, and in the working as well, the old orders of chivalry or knighthood strongly commend themselves, for here there was, in principle, both the maintenance of high ideals of honour courtesy and ***noblesse oblige,*** and the rendering of chivalrous service. Chesterton has put it well in the phrase "the giving things which cannot be demanded, the avoiding things which cannot be punished." Moreover, admission to the orders of knighthood was free to all provided there were that cause which came from personal character alone. Knighthood was the crown of knightly service and it was forfeited for recreancy. Is there not in this some suggestion of what may again be established as an incentive and a reward, and as well, as a vital agency for the reorganization of society?

Knighthood is personal, and is for the lifetime of the recipient. Is there any value in an estate where status is heritable? If there is any validity in the theory of varying and persistent race-values, it would seem so, yet the idea of recognizing this excellence of certain families and the reasonable probability of their maintaining the established standard unimpaired, and so giving them a formal status, would no doubt be repugnant to the vast majority of men in the United States. I think this aversion is based on prejudice, natural but ill-founded. We resent the idea of privilege without responsibility, as we should, but this, while it was the condition of those aristocracies which were operative at the time of the founding of the Republic, was opposed to the Mediaeval, or true idea, which linked responsibility with privilege. The old privilege is gone and cannot be restored, but already we have a new privilege which is being claimed and enforced by proletarian groups, and the legislative representatives of the whole people stand in such terror of massed votes that they not only fail to check this astonishing and topsy-turvy movement, but actually further its pretensions. The "dictatorship of the proletariat" actually means the restoration of privilege in a form far more tyrannical and monstrous than any ever exercised by the old aristocracies of Italy, France, Germany and England. Much recent legislation in Washington exempting certain industrial and agricultural classes from the operation of laws which bear heavily on other classes, and some of the claims and pretensions of unionized labor, tend in precisely the same direction.

It is not restoration of privilege I have in mind but rather in a sense the prevention of this through the existence of a class or estate that has a fixed status dependent first on character and service and then on an assured position that is not contingent on political favour, the bulk of votes, or the acquisition of an inordinate amount of money. Surety of position works towards independence of thought and action and towards strong leadership. It establishes and maintains certain high ideals of honour, chivalry, and service as well as of courtesy and manners. If the things for which the gentlemen, the knighthood and the nobility of Europe during the Christian dispensation were responsible were stricken from the record there would be comparatively little left of the history of European culture and civilization.

After all, is it merely sentimentalism and a sense of the picturesque that leads us to look backward with some wistfulness to the days of which the record is still left us in legends and fairy-tales and old romance, when ignorance and vulgarity did not sit in high places even if arrogance and pride and tyranny sometimes did, and when the profiteer and the oriental financier and the successful politician did not represent the distinction and the chivalry and the courtesy and the honour of the social organism man builds for his own habitation? The idea of knighthood still stirs us and the deeds of chivalry and the courtesy and the honour of the social Knights of the Round Table, Crusaders and knights errant, the quest of the Holy Grail, rescue and adventure, the fighting with paynims and powers of evil, still stir our blood and arouse in our minds strange contrasts and antinomies. Princes and fair chatelaines in their wide domains with castle and chase and delicate pleasaunce, liegemen bound to them by more than the feudal ties of service. All the varied honours of nobility, vitalized by significant ritual and symbolized by splendid and beautiful costumes. Courts of Love and troubadours and trouveres, kings who were kings indeed, with the splendour and courtesy and beneficence of their courts--Louis the Saint and Frederic II, Edward III and King Charles--above all the simple rank and high honour of the "gentleman," the representative of a long line of honourable tradition, no casual and purse-proud upstart, but of proud race and unquestioned status, proud because it stood for certain high ideals of honour and chivalry and loyalty, of courtesy and breeding and compassion. All these old things of long ago still rouse in us answering humours, and there are a few of us who can hardly see just why they are inconsistent with liberty and opportunity, justice, righteousness and mercy.

Somehow the last two generations, and especially the last ten years, have revealed many things hitherto hidden, and as we envisage society as it has come to be, estimating it by new-found standards and establishing new comparisons through a recovery of a more just historical sense, the question comes whether it is indeed more wholesome, more beautiful, more normal to man as he is, than the older society that in varying forms but always the same principle, had held throughout all history until the new model came in, now hardly a century ago.

I do not think this wistful and bewildered looking backward is particularly due to a new desire for beauty, that comeliness of condition that existed then and has now given place to gross ugliness and ill-conditioned manners and ways. Rather it seems to me it is due to a sense of irrationality and fundamental injustice in the present order, coupled with a new terror of the proximate issue as this already is revealing itself amongst many peoples. We resent the high estate, purchasable and purchased, of the cynical intriguer and the vulgar profiteer, of the tradesman in "big business," the cheap prophet and the pathetic progeny of "successful men" fast reverting to type. We know our city councils and our state legislatures and our houses of congress, we know our newspapers, their standards and the motive powers behind them, and what they record of the character and the doings of what they call "society men and women." Above all we know that under the ancient regime, in spite of manifold failures, shortcomings and disloyalty, there was such a thing as a standard of honour, a principle of chivalry, an impulse to unselfish service, a criterion of courtesy and good manners; we look for these things now in vain, except amongst those little enclaves of oblivion where the old character and old breeding still maintain a fading existence, and as we consider what we have become we sometimes wonder if the price we have paid for "democracy" was not too extortionate.

Above all, we are tempted to this query when we think of our vanishing standards of right and wrong, of our progressive reversal of values, of our diminishing stock of social character. We tore down in indignant revolt the rotten fabric of a bad social system when it had so far declined from its ideal and its former estate that it could no longer be endured, and we made a new thing, full as we were with the fire of desire for a new righteousness and a new system that would compass it. Perhaps we did well, at least we hardly could have done anything else; but now we are again in the position of our forefathers who saw things as they were and acted with force and decision. There are as many counts against our society of plutocrats, politicians and proletarians, mingled in complete and ineffective confusion, as there were against the aristocracies, so called, of the eighteenth century. Perhaps there are more, at least many of them are different, but the indictment is no less sweeping.

Our plan, so generous, so liberal, so high-minded in many ways, has failed to produce the results we desired, while it has worked itself out to the point of menace. It is for us to see these facts clearly, and so to act, and so promptly, that we may not have to await the destroying force of cataclysm for the correction of our errors.

IV
THE INDUSTRIAL PROBLEM

The solution of the industrial and economic problem that now confronts the entire world with an insistence that is not to be denied, is contingent on the restoration, first of all, of the holiness and the joy of work. Labour is not a curse, it is rather one of the greatest of the earthly blessings of man, provided its sanctity is recognized and its performance is accomplished with satisfaction to the labourer. In work man creates, whether the product is a bushel of potatoes from a space of once arid ground, or whether it is the Taj Mahal, Westminster Abbey or the Constitution of the United States, and so working he partakes something of the divine power of creation.

When work is subject to slavery, all sense of its holiness is lost, both by master and bondman; when it is subject to the factory system all the joy in labour is lost. Ingenuity may devise one clever panacea after another for the salving work and for lifting the working classes from the intolerable conditions that have prevailed for more than a century; they will be ephemeral in their existence and futile in their results unless sense of holiness is restored, and the joy in production and creation given back to those who have been defrauded.

Before Christianity prevailed slavery was universal in civilized communities, labour, as conducted under that regime, was a curse, and this at length came home to roost on the gaunt wreckage of imperialism. Thereafter came slowly increasing liberty under the feudal system with its small social units and its system of production for use not profits, monasticism with its doctrine and practice of the sanctity of work, and the Church with its progressive emancipation of the spiritual part of man. Work was not easy, on the contrary it was very hard throughout the Dark Ages and Mediaevalism, but there is no particular merit in easy work. It was virtually free except for the labour and contributions in kind exacted by the over-lord (less in proportion than taxes in money have been at several times since) from the workers on the soil, and in the crafts of every kind redeemed from undue arduousness by the joy that comes from doing a thing well and producing something of beauty, originality and technical perfection.

The period during which work possessed the most honourable status and the joy in work was the greatest, extends from the beginnings of the twelfth century well into the sixteenth. In some centuries, and along certain lines of activity, it continued much longer, notably in England and the United States, but social and industrial conditions were rapidly changing, the old aristocracy was becoming perverted, Lutheranisms, Calvinism and Puritanism were breaking down the old communal sense of brotherhood so arduously built up during the Middle Ages, capitalism was ousting the trade and craft guilds of free labour and political absolutism was crushing ever lower and lower a proletariat that was fast losing the last vestiges of old liberty. The fact of slavery without the name was gradually imposed on the agricultural classes, and after the suppression of the monasteries in England work as work lost its sacred character and fell under contempt. With the outbreak of industrialism in the last quarter of the eighteenth century through the institution and introduction of "labour-saving" machinery and the consequent division of labour, the factory system, the joint-stock company and capitalism, this new slavery was extended to industrial workers, and with its establishment disappeared the element of joy in labour.

For fifty years, about the blackest half-century civilization has had to record, this condition of industrial slavery continued with little amendment. Very slowly, however, the workers themselves, championed by certain aristocrats like the seventh Earl of Shaftsbury against professional Liberals like Cobden, Bright, and Gladstone in England, began to loosen the shackles that bound them to infamous conditions, and after the abrogation of laws that made any association of workingmen a penal offense, the labour unions began to ameliorate certain of the servile conditions under which for two generations the workman had suffered. Since then the process of abolishing wage-slavery went slowly forward until at last the war came not only to threaten its destruction altogether but also to place the emancipated workers in a position where they could dictate terms and conditions to capital, to employers, to government and to the general public; while even now in many parts of Europe and America, besides Russia, overt attempts are being made to bring back the old slavery, only with the former bondsmen in supreme dictatorship, the former employers and the "bourgeoisie" in the new serfage.

The old slavery is gone, but the joy in work has not been restored; instead, those who have achieved triumphant emancipation turn from labour itself with the same distaste, yes, with greater aversion than that which obtained under the old regime. With every added liberty and exemption, with every shortening of hours and increase of pay, production per hour falls off and the quality of the output declines. What is the reason for this? Is it due to the viciousness of the worker, to his natural selfishness, greed and cruelty? I do not think so, but rather that the explanation is to be found in the fact that the industrial system of modernism has resulted in a condition where the joy has been altogether cut out of labour, and that until this state of things has been reversed and the sense of the holiness of work and the joy of working have been restored, it is useless to look for workable solutions of the labour problem. The *fact* of industrial slavery has been done away with but the sense of the servile condition that attaches to work has been retained, therefore the idea of the dignity and holiness of labour has not come back any more than the old joy and satisfaction. Failing this recovery, no reorganization of industrial relations, neither profit-sharing nor shop committees, neither nationalization nor state socialism, neither the abolition of capital, nor Soviets nor syndicalism nor the dictatorship of the proletariat will get us anywhere. It is all a waste of time, and, through its ultimate failure and disappointments, an intensification of an industrial disease.

Why is it that this is so? For an answer I must probe deep and, it may seem, cut wildly. I believe it is because we have built up a system that goes far outside the limits of human scale, transcends human capacity, is forbidden by the laws and conditions of life, and must be abrogated if it is not to destroy itself and civilization in the process.

What, precisely has taken place? Late in the eighteenth century two things happened; the discovery of the potential inherent in coal and its derivative, steam, with electricity yet unexploited but ready to hand, and the application of this to industrial purposes, together with the initiating of a long and astounding series of discoveries and inventions all applicable to industrial purposes. With a sort of vertiginous rapidity the whole industrial process was transformed from what it had been during the period of recorded history; steam and machinery took the place of brain and hand power directly applied, and a revolution greater than any other was effected.

The new devices were hailed as "labour-saving" but they vastly increased labour both in hours of work and in hands employed. Bulk production through the factory system was inevitable, the result being an enormous surplus over the normal and local demand. To organize and conduct these processes of bulk-production required money greater in amount than individuals could furnish; so grew up capitalism, the joint-stock company, credit and cosmopolitan finance. To produce profits and dividends markets must be found for the huge surplus product. This was accomplished by stimulating the covetousness of people for things they had not thought of, under normal conditions would not, in many cases, need, and very likely would be happier without, and in "dumping" on supposedly barbarous peoples in remote parts of the world, articles alien to their traditions and their mode of life and generally pestiferous in their influence and results. So came advertising in all its branches, direct and indirect, from the newspaper and the bill-board to the drummer, the diplomatic representative and the commercial missionary.

Every year saw some new invention that increased the product per man, the development of some new advertising device, the conquest of some new territory or the delimitation of some new "sphere of influence," and the revelation of some new possibility in the covetousness of man. Profits rose to new heights and accumulating dividends clamoured for new opportunities for investment. Competition tended to cut down returns, therefore labour was more and more sustained through diminished wages and laws that savagely prevented any concerted effort towards self-defense. Improvements in agricultural processes and the application of machinery and steam power, together with bulk-production and scientific localization of crops, threw great quantities of farm-labourers out of work and drove them into the industrial towns, while advances in medical science and in sanitation raised the proportion of births to deaths and soon provided a surplus of potential labour so that the operation of the "law of supply and demand," extolled by a new philosophy and enforced by the new "representative" or democratic and parliamentary government, resulted in an unfailing supply of cheap labour paid wages just beyond the limit of starvation.

At last there came evidences that the limit had been reached; the whole world had been opened up and pre-empted, labour was beginning to demand and even get more adequate wages, competition, once hailed as "the life of trade" was becoming so fierce that dividends were dwindling. Something had to be done and in self-defense industries began to coalesce in enormous "trusts" and "combines" and monopolies. Capitalization of millions now ran into billions, finance became international in its scope and gargantuan in its proportions and ominousness, advertising grew from its original simplicity and naivete into a vast industry based on all that the most ingenious professors could tell of applied psychology, subsidizing artists, poets, men of letters, employing armies of men along a hundred different lines, expending millions annually in its operations, making the modern newspaper possible, and ultimately developing the whole system of propaganda which has now become the one great determining factor in the making of public opinion.

When the twentieth century opened, that industrialism which had begun just a century before, had, with its various collateral developments, financial, educational, journalistic, etc., become not only the greatest force in society, but as well a thing operating on the largest scale that man had ever essayed: beside it the Roman Empire was parochial.

The result of this institution, conceived on such imperial lines, was, in the field we are now considering, the total destruction of the sense of the holiness of labour and of joy in work. It extended far beyond the limits of pure industrialism; it moulded and controlled society in all its forms, destroying ideals old as history, reversing values, confusing issues and wrecking man's powers of judgment. Until the war it seemed irresistible, now its weakness and the fallacy of its assumptions are revealed, but it has become so absolutely a part of our life, indeed of our nature, that we are unable to estimate it by any sound standards of judgment, and even when we approximate this we cannot think in other terms when we try to devise our schemes of redemption. Even the socialist and the Bolshevik think in imperial terms when they try to compass the ending of imperialism.

Under this supreme system, as I see it, the two essential things I have spoken of cannot be restored, nor could they maintain themselves if, by some miracle, they were once re-established. The indictment cannot be closed here. The actual condition that has developed from industrialism presents certain factors that are not consonant with sane, wholesome and Christian living. Not only has the unit of human scale in human society been done away with, not only have the sense of the nobility of work and joy in the doing been exterminated, but, as well, certain absolutely false principles and methods have been adopted which are not susceptible of reform but only of abolition.

Of some of these I have spoken already; the alarming drift towards cities, until now in the United States more than one-half the population is urban; the segregation of industries in certain cities and regions; the minute division of labour and intensive specialization; the abnormal growth of a true proletariat or non-landholding class; the flooding of the country by cheap labour drawn from the most backward communities and from peoples of low race-value. Out of this has arisen a bitter class conflict and the ominous beginnings of a perilous class consciousness, with actual warfare joined in several countries, and threatened in all others where industrial civilization is prevalent. With this has grown up an artificially stimulated covetousness for a thousand futile luxuries, and a standard of living that presupposes a thousand non-essentials as basic necessities. Production for profit, not use, excess production due to machinery, efficient organization, and surplus of labour, together with the necessity for marketing the product at a profit, have produced a state of things where at least one-half the available labour in the country is engaged in the production and sale of articles which are not necessary to physical, intellectual or spiritual life, while of the remainder, hardly more than a half is employed in production, the others are devoting themselves to distribution and to the war of competition through advertising and the capturing of trade by ingenious and capable salesmen. It is a significant fact that two of the greatest industries in the United States are the making of automobiles and moving pictures.

It is probably true to say that of the potential labour in the United States, about one-fourth is producing those things which are physically, intellectually and spiritually necessary; the remaining three-fourths are essentially non-producers: they must, however, be housed, fed, clothed, and amused, and the cost of this support is added to the cost of the necessities of life. The reason for the present high cost of living lies possibly here.

Lest I be misunderstood, let me say here that under the head of necessities of life I do not mean a new model automobile each year, moving pictures, mechanical substitutes for music or any other art, and the thousand catch-trade devices that appear each year for the purpose of filching business from another or establishing a new desire in the already over-crowded imaginations of an over-stimulated populace. Particularly do I not mean advertising in any sense in which it is now understood and practised. If, as I believe to be the case, production for profit, rather than for use, the reversal of the ancient doctrine that the demand must produce the supply, in favour of the doctrine that the supply must foster the demand, is the foundation of our economic error and our industrial ills, then it follows that advertising as it is now carried on by billboards, circulars and newspapers, by drummers, solicitors and consular agents, falls in the same condemnation, for except by its offices the system could not have succeeded or continue to function. It is bad in itself as the support and strength of a bad institution, but its guilt does not stop here. So plausible is it, so essential to the very existence of the contemporary regime, so knit up with all the commonest affairs of life, so powerful in its organization and broad in its operations, it has poisoned, and continues to poison, the minds of men so that the headlong process of losing all sense of comparative values is accelerated, while every instinctive effort at recovery and readjustment is nullified. How far this process has gone may be illustrated by two instances. It is only a few months ago that a most respected clergyman publicly declared that missionaries were the greatest and most efficient asset to trade because they were unofficial commercial agents who opened up new and savage countries to Western commerce through advertising commodities of which the natives had never heard, and arousing in them a sense of acquisitiveness that meant more wealth and business for trade and manufacture, which should support foreign missions on this ground at least. More recently the head of an advertising concern in New York is reported to have said: "It is principally through advertising that we have arrived at the high degree of civilization which this age enjoys, for advertising has taught us the use of books and how to furnish our homes with the thousand and one comforts that add so materially to our physical and intellectual well-being. The future of the world depends on advertising. Advertising is the salvation of civilization, for civilization cannot outlive advertising a century."

It is tempting to linger over such a delectable morsel as this, for even if it is only the absurd and irresponsible output of one poor, foolish man, it does express more or less what industrial civilization holds to be true, though few would avow their faith so whole-heartedly. The statement was made as propaganda, and propaganda is merely advertising in its most insidious and dangerous form. The thing revealed its possibilities during the war, but the black discredit that was then very justly attached to it could not prevail against its manifest potency, and it is now universally used after the most comprehensive and frequently unscrupulous fashion, with results that can only be perilous in the extreme. The type and calibre of mind that has now been released from long bondage, and by weight of numbers is now fast taking over the direction of affairs, is curiously subservient to the written word, and lacking a true sense of comparative values, without effective leadership either secular or religious, is easily swayed by every wind of doctrine. The forces of evil that are ever in conflict with the forces of right are notoriously ingenious in making the worse appear the better cause, and with every desire for illumination and for following the right way, the multitude, whether educated or illiterate, fall into the falsehoods of others' imaginings. Money, efficiency, an acquired knowledge of mob psychology, the printing press and the mail service acting in alliance, and directed by fanatical or cynical energy, form a force of enormous potency that is now being used effectively throughout society. It is irresponsible, anonymous and pervasive. Through its operation the last barriers are broken down between the leadership of character and the leadership of craft, while all formal distinctions between the valuable and the valueless are swept away.

I have spoken at some length of this particular element in the present condition of things, because in both its aspects, as the support of our present industrial and economic system and as the efficient moulder of a fluid and unstable public opinion, it is perhaps the strongest and most subtle force of which we must take account.

With a system so prevalent as imperial industry, so knit up with every phase of life and thought, and so determining a factor in all our concepts, united as it is with two such invincible allies as advertising and propaganda, it is inconceivable that it should be overthrown by any human force from without. Holding it to be essentially wrong, it seems to me providential that it is already showing signs of falling by its own weight. Production of commodities has far exceeded production of the means of payment, and society is now running on promises to pay, on paper obligations, on anticipations of future production and sale, on credit, in a word. The war has enormously magnified this condition until an enforced liquidation would mean bankruptcy for all the nations of the earth, while the production of utilities is decreasing in proportion to the production of luxuries, labour is exacting increasing pay for decreasing hours of work and quality of output, and the enormous financial structure, elaborately and ingeniously built up through several generations, is in grave danger of immediate catastrophe. The whole world is in the position of an insolvent debtor who is so deeply involved that his creditors cannot afford to let him go into bankruptcy, and so keep him out of the Poor Debtor's Court by doling out support from day to day. Confidence is the only thing that keeps matters going; what happens when this is lost is now being demonstrated in many parts of Europe. The optimist claims that increased production, coupled with enforced economy, will produce a satisfactory solution, but there is no evidence that labour, now having the whip-hand, will give up its present advantage sufficiently to make this possible; even if it did, payment must be in the form of exchange or else in further promises to pay, while the capacity of the world for consumption is limited somewhere, though thus far "big business" has failed to recognize this fact. At present the interest charges on debts, both public and private, have reached a point where they come near to consuming all possible profits even from a highly accelerated rate of production. Altogether it is reasonable to assume that the present financial-industrial system is near its term for reasons inherent in itself, let alone the possibility of a further extension of the drastic and completely effective measures of destruction that are characteristics of Bolshevism and its blood-brothers.

Assuming that this is so, two questions arise: what is to take the place of imperial industry, and how is this substitution to be brought about?

I think the answer to the first is: a social and industrial system based on small, self-contained, largely self-sufficing units, where supply follows demand, where production is primarily for use not profit, and where in all industrial operations some system will obtain which is more or less that of the guilds of the Middle Ages. I should like to go into this a little more in detail before trying to answer the second question.

The normal social unit is a group of families predominantly of the same race, territorially compact, of substantially the same ideals as expressed in religion and the philosophy of life, and sufficiently numerous to provide from within itself the major part of those things which are necessary to physical, intellectual and spiritual well-being. It should consist of a central nucleus of houses, each with its garden, the churches, schools and public buildings that are requisite, the manufactories and workshops that supply the needs of the community, the shops for sale of those things not produced at home, and all necessary places of amusement. Around this residential centre should be sufficient agricultural land to furnish all the farm products that will be consumed by the community itself. The nucleus of habitation and industry, together with the surrounding farms, make up the social unit, which is to the fullest possible degree, self-contained, self-sufficient and self-governing.

Certain propositions are fundamental, and they are as follows: Every family should own enough land to support itself at need. The farms included in the unit must produce enough to meet the needs of the population. Industry must be so organized that it will normally serve the resident population along every feasible line. Only such things as cannot be produced at home on account of climatic or soil limitations should be imported from outside. All necessary professional services should be obtainable within the community itself. All financial transactions such as loans, credits, banking and insurance should be domestic. Surplus products, whether agricultural, industrial or professional, should be considered as by-products, and in no case should the producing agency acquire such magnitude that home-consumption becomes a side issue and production for profit take the place of production for use.

All this is absolutely opposed to our present system, but our present system is wasteful, artificial, illogical, unsocial, and therefore vicious. I have said enough as to the falsities, the dangers and the failures of bulk-production through the operations of capitalism, the factory system and advertising, but its concomitant, the segregation of industries, is equally objectionable. To ship hogs 1,500 miles to be slaughtered and packed in food form, and then ship this manufactured product back to the source from which the raw material came; to feed a great city with grain, potatoes and fruits coming from 1,000 to 3,000 miles away, and vegetables from a distance of several hundred miles, while the farms within a radius of fifty miles are abandoned and barren; to make all the shoes for the nation in one small area, to spin the wool and cotton and weave the cloth in two or three others; to make the greater part of the furniture in one state, the automobiles in a second and the breakfast food in a third, is so preposterous a proposition that it belongs in Gulliver's Travels, not in the annals of a supposedly intelligent people. The only benefit is that which for a time accrued to the railways, which carted raw materials and finished products back and forth over thousands of miles of their lines, the costs of shipment and reshipment being naturally added to the price to the consumer. The penalties for this uneconomic procedure were borne by society at large, not only in the increased costs but through the abnormal communities, each with its tens of thousands of operatives all engaged in the same work and generally drawn from foreign races (with the active co-operation of the steamship lines), and the permanent dislocation of the labour supply, together with the complete disruption of the social synthesis.

With production for profit and segregation of industries has come an almost infinitesimal division and specialization of labour. Under a right industrial system this would be reduced, not magnified. The dignity of labour and the joy of creation demand that in so far as possible each man should carry through one entire operation. This is of course now, and always has been under any highly developed civilization, impossible in practice, except along certain lines of art and craftsmanship. The evils of the existing system can in a measure be done away with the moment production for use is the recognized law, for it is only in bulk-production that this intensive specialization can be made to pay. Bulk-production there will always be until, and if, the world is reorganized on the basis of an infinite number of self-contained social units, but in the ideal community--and I am dealing now with ideals--it would not exist.

Allied with this is the whole question of the factory method and the use and misuse of machinery. It seems to me that the true principle is that machinery and the factory are admissible only when so employed they actually do produce, in bulk operations, a better product, and with less labour, than is possible through hand work. Weaving, forging and all work where human action must be more or less mechanical, offer a fair field for the machine and the factory, but wherever the human element can enter, where personality and the skilled craft of the hand are given play, the machine and the factory are inadmissible. The great city, creation of "big business," segregation of industries, advertising, salesmanship and a hundred other concomitants of modernism, have built up an abnormal and avaricious demand for bulk-production along lines where the handicraft should function. It becomes necessary--let us say--to provide a million dollars worth of furniture for a ten million dollar hotel (itself to be superseded and scrapped in perhaps ten years) and naturally only the most intensive and efficient factory system can meet this demand. Rightly, however, the furniture of a community should be produced by the local cabinet makers, and so it should be in many other industries now entirely taken over by the factory system.

For the future then we must consciously work for the building upward from primary units, so completely reversing our present practice of creating the big thing and fighting hopelessly to preserve such small and few doles of liberty and personality as may be permitted to filter downward from above. This is the only true democracy, and the thing we call by the name is not this, largely because we have bent our best energies to the building up of vast and imperial aggregates which have inevitably assumed a complete unity in themselves and become dominating, tyrannical and ruthless forces that have operated regardless of the sound laws and wholesome principles of a right society. Neither the vital democracy of principle nor the artificial democracy of practice can exist in conjunction with imperialism, whether this is established in government, in industry, in trade, in society or in education.

If we can assume, then, the gradual development of a new society in which these principles will be carried out, a society that is made up of social units of human scale, self-contained, self-supporting and self-governed, where production is primarily for use not profit, and where bulk-production is practically non-existent, the sub-division of labour reduced to the lowest practicable point, machinery employed to a much less extent than now, and the factory system abolished, what organic form will labour take on in place of that which now obtains? It is possible to forecast this only in the most general terms, for life itself must operate to determine the lines of development and dictate the consequent forms. If we can acquire a better standard of comparative values, and with a clearer and more fearless vision estimate the rights and wrongs of the contemporary system, rejecting the ill thing and jealously preserving, or passionately regaining, the good, we shall be able to establish certain broad, fundamental and governing principles, and doing this we can await in confidence the evolution of the organic forms that will be the working agencies of the new society.

I have tried to indicate some of the basic principles of a new society. The operating forms, so far as industry is concerned, will, I think, follow in essential respects the craft-guilds of the Middle Ages. They will not be an archaeological restoration, as some of the English protagonists of this great revolution seem to anticipate, they will be variously adapted to the peculiar conditions of a new century, but the basic principles will be preserved. Whatever happens, I am sure it will not be either a continuation of the present system of capitalism and profit-hunting, or nationalization of industries, or state socialism in any form, or anything remotely resembling Bolshevism, syndicalism or a "dictatorship of the proletariat." Here, as in government, education and social relations, the power and the authority of the state must decline, government itself withdrawing more and more from interference with the operation of life, and liberty find its way back to the individual and to the social and economic groups. We live now under a more tyrannical and inquisitorial regime, in spite of (partly perhaps because of) its democratic forms and dogmas, than is common in historical records. Nationalization or state socialism would mean so great a magnifying of this condition that existence would soon become both grotesque and intolerable. We must realize, and soon, that man may lose even the last semblance of liberty, as well under a nominal democracy as under a nominal despotism or theocracy.

The guild system was the solution of the industrial problem offered and enforced by Christianity working through secular life; it presupposed the small social and industrial unit and becomes meaningless if conceived in the gigantic and comprehensive scale of modern institutions. "National guilds" is a contradiction in terms: it takes on the same element of error that inheres in the idea of "one big union." In certain respects the Christian guild resembled the modern trade union, but it differed from it in more ways, and it seems to be true that wherever this difference exists the guild was right and the union is wrong. Community of fellowship and action amongst men of each craft trade or calling is essential under any social system, good or bad, and it would be inseparable from the better society that must sometime grow up on the basis of the unit of human scale, for these autonomous groups, in order to furnish substantially all that their component parts could require, would have to be of considerable size as compared with the little farming villages of New England, though in contrast with the great cities of modernism they would be small indeed. In these new "walled towns" there would be enough men engaged in agriculture, in the necessary industrial occupations, in trade and in the professions to form many guilds of workable size, and normally these guilds would neither contain members of two or more professions or occupations, nor those from outside the community itself. The guild cannot function under intensive methods of production or where production is primarily for profit, or where the factory system prevails, or where capitalism is the established system, or under combinations, trusts or other devices for the establishing and maintenance of great aggregates tending always towards monopoly. However much we may admire the guild system and desire its restoration, we may as well recognize this fact at once. The imperial scale must go and the human scale be restored before the guild can come back in any general sense.

I am assuming that this will happen, either through conscious action on the part of the people or as the result of catastrophe that always overtakes those who remain wedded to the illusions of falsity. On this assumption what are these enduring principles that will control the guild system of industry in the new State, however may be its form?

The answer is to be found in the old guilds, altars, shrines, vestments and sacred vessels were given in incredible quantities for the furnishing and embellishment of the chapel or church; funds also for the maintenance of priestly offices especially dedicated to the guild.

Closely allied with the religious spirit was that of good-fellowship and merry-making. Every sort of feast and game and pageant was a part of the guild system, as it was indeed of life generally at this time when men did not have to depend upon hired professional purveyors of amusement for their edification. What they wanted they did themselves, and this community in worship and community in merry-making did more even than the merging of common material interests, to knit the whole body together into a living organism.

In how far the old system can be revived and put into operation is a question. Certainly it cannot be adopted as a fad and imposed on an unwilling society as a clever archaeological restoration. It will have to grow naturally out of life itself and along lines at present hardly predicable. There are many evidences that just this spontaneous generation is taking place. The guild system is being preached widely in England where the defects of the present scheme are more obvious and the resulting labour situation--or rather social situation--is more fraught with danger than elsewhere, and already the restoration seems to have made considerable headway. I am convinced, however, that the vital aspects of the case are primarily due to the interior working of a new spirit born of disillusionment and the undying fire in man that flames always towards regeneration; what the ardent preaching of the enthusiastic protagonists of the crusade best accomplishes is the creation in the minds of those not directly associated with the movement of a readiness to give sympathy and support to the actual accomplishment when it manifests itself. Recently I have come in contact here in America with several cases where the workmen themselves have broken away from the old ways and have actually established what are to all intents and purposes craft-guilds, without in the least realizing that they were doing this.

I think the process is bound to continue, for the old order has broken down and is so thoroughly discredited it can hardly be restored. If time is granted us, great things must follow, but it is increasingly doubtful if this necessary element of time can be counted on. Daily the situation grows more menacing. Capital, which so long exploited labour to its own fabulous profit, is not disposed to sit quiet while the fruits of its labours and all prospects of future emoluments are being dissipated, and it is hard at work striving to effect a "return to normalcy." In this it is being unconsciously aided by the bulk of union labour which, encouraged by the paramount position it achieved during the war, influenced by an avarice it may well have learned from its former masters, as narrow in its vision as they, and increasingly subservient to a leadership which is frequently cynical and unscrupulous and always of an order of character and intelligence which is tending to lower and lower levels, is alienating sympathy and bringing unionism into disrepute. In the United States the tendency is steadily towards a very dangerous reactionism, with a corresponding strengthening of the radical element which aims at revolution, and that impossible thing, a proletarian dictatorship. It is this latter which is rampant and at present unchecked in Europe, and this also is a constant menace to the success of those sane and righteous movements which take their lead from the guild system of the Middle Ages. A third danger, but one which is constantly on the decline at present, partly because of the general disrepute of governments and partly because of the enormous accessions of power now accruing both to reactionism and radical revolutionism, or

"Bolshevism," is state socialism or nationalization, which leaves untouched all the fatal elements in industrialism while it changes only the agents of administration. The complete collapse of able and constructive and righteous leadership, which is one of the startling phenomena of modernism, has left uncontrolled the enormous energy that has been released during the last three generations, and this is working blindly but effectively towards a cataclysm so precipitate and comprehensive that it is impossible not to fear that it may determine long before the sober and informed elements in society have accomplished very much in the recovery and establishment of sound and righteous principles and methods.

Of course we can compass whichever result we will. We may shut our eyes to the omens and let matters drift to disaster, or we may take thought and council and avert the penalty that threatens us; the event is in our own hands. It is as criminal to foresee and predict only catastrophe as it is to compass this through lethargy, selfishness and illusion. We are bound to believe that righteousness will prevail, even in our own time, and believing this, what, in general terms will be the construction of the new system that must take the place of industrialism?

I have already indicated what seem to me the fundamental ideas as: the small social unit that is self-sustaining; production primarily for use, cooeperation in place of competition; a revived guild system with the abolition of capitalism, exploitation and intensive specialization as we now know these dominant factors in modern civilization. In the application of these principles there are certain innovations that will, I think, take place, and these may be listed somewhat as follows:

Land holding will become universal and the true proletariat or landless class will disappear. It may be that the holding of land will become a prerequisite to active citizenship. Industrial production being for use not profit, the great city becomes a thing of the past, and life is rendered simpler through the elimination of a thousand useless and vicious luxuries; those employed in mechanical industries will be incalculably fewer than now, while those that remain will give only a portion of their time to industrial production, the remainder being available for productive work on their own gardens and farms. The handicrafts will be restored to their proper place and dignity, taking over into creative labour large numbers of those who otherwise would be sacrificed to the factory system. Where bulk production, as in weaving and the preparation and manufacturing of metals, is economical and unavoidable and carried on by factory methods, these manufactories will probably be taken over by the several communities (not by the state as a whole) and administered as public institutions for the benefit of the community and under conditions and regulations which ensure justice and well-being to the employees. All those in any community engaged in a given occupation, as for example, building, will form one guild made up of masters, journeymen and apprentices, with the same principles and much the same methods as prevailed under the ancient guild system. Fluctuating scales of prices determined by fluctuating conditions of competition, supply and demand, and power of coercion, will give place to "the fair price" fixed by concerted community action and revised from time to time in order to preserve a right balance with the general scale of cost of raw materials and cost of living. A maximum of returns in the shape of profits or dividends will be fixed by law. The community itself will undertake the furnishing of credits, loans and necessary capital for the establishing of a new business, charging a small rate of interest and maintaining a reserve fund to meet these operations. Private banking, insurance and the loaning of money on collateral will cease to exist.

I dare say this will all sound chimerical and irrational in the extreme; I do not see it in that light. Its avowed object is the supersession of "big business" in all its phases by something that comes down to human scale. It aims to reduce labour and divide it more evenly by making the great mass of non-producers--those engaged in distribution, salesmanship, advertising, propaganda, and the furnishing of things unnecessary to the bodily, intellectual and spiritual needs of man--actual producers and self-supporting to a very large extent. It aims at restoring to work some sense of the joy in creation through active mind and hand. It aims at the elimination of the parasitic element in society and of that dangerous factor which subsists on wealth it acquires without earning, and by sheer force of its own opulence dominates and degrades society. It does not strike at private ownership, but rather exalts, extends and defends this, but it ***does*** cut into all the theories and practices of communism and socialism by establishing the principle and practice of fellowship and cooeperation. Is this "chimerical and irrational"?

Meanwhile the "walled towns" do not exist and may not for generations. "Big business" is indisposed to abrogate itself. Trade unionism is fighting for its life and thereafter for world conquest, while the enmity between capital and labour increases, with no evidence that a restored guild system is even approximately ready to take its place. Strikes and lockouts grow more and more numerous, and wider and more menacing in their scope. The day of the "general strike" has only been delayed at the eleventh hour in several countries, and a general strike, if it can hold for a sufficient period, means, where-ever it occurs and whenever it succeeds, the end of civilization and the loosing of the floods of anarchy. There is hardly time for us patiently to await the slow process of individual and corporate enlightenment or the spontaneous development of the autonomous communities which, if they were sufficient in number, would solve the problem through eliminating the danger. What then, in the premises, can we do?

There are of course certain concrete things which might help, as for instance the further extension and honest trying out of the "Kansas plan" for regulating industrial relations; the forming of "consumers leagues," and all possible support and furtherance of cooeperative efforts of every sort. There are further possibilities (perhaps hardly probabilities) of controlling stock issues and stock holdings so that dividends do not have to be paid on grossly inflated capitalization, and fixing the maximum of dividends payable to non-active stockholders. Equally desirable but equally improbable, is the raising of the level of leadership in the labour unions so that these valuable institutions may no longer stultify themselves and wreck their own cause by their unjust and anti-social regulations as to apprentices, control of maximum output and its standard of quality, division of labour with ironclad inhibitions against one man doing another's work and against one man doing what six men can do less well, and as to the obligation to strike on order when no local or personal grievance exists. Most useful of all would be a voluntary renunciation, on the part of the purchasing public, of nine-tenths of the futile luxuries they now insanely demand, coupled with the production by themselves of some of the commodities which are easily producable; in other words, establishing some measure of self-support and so releasing many men and women from the curse of existence under factory conditions and giving them an opportunity of living a normal life under self-supporting circumstances. This, coupled with a fostering of the "back to the farm" movement, and the development of conditions which would make this process more practicable and the life more attractive, would do much, though in small ways, towards producing a more wholesome and less threatening state of affairs.

Back of the whole problem, however, lies a fallacy in our conception of existence that must be eliminated before even the most constructive panaceas can possibly work. I mean the whole doctrine of natural rights which has become the citadel of capitalism in all its most offensive aspects, and of labour in its most insolent assumptions. The "rights" of property, the "right" to strike, the "right" to collective bargaining, the "right" to shut down an essential industry or to "walk out" and then picket the place so that it may not be reopened, the "right" to vote and hold office and do any fool thing you please so long as it is within the law, these are applications of what I mean when I speak of a gross fallacy that has come into being and has stultified our intelligence while bringing near the wrecking of our whole system.

Neither man nor his community possesses any ***absolute*** rights; they are all conditioned on how they are exercised. If they are not so conditioned they become privilege, which is a right not subject to conditions, and privilege is one of the things republicanism and democracy and every other effort towards human emancipation have set themselves up to destroy. Even the "right to life, liberty and the pursuit of happiness" is conditioned by the manner of use, and the same is true of every other and unspecified right. I do not propose to speak here of more than one aspect of this self-evident truth, but the single instance I cite is one that bears closely on the question of our industrial and economic situation; it is the responsibility to society of property or capital on the one hand and of labour on the other, when both invoke their "rights" to justify them in oppressing the general public in the pursuit of their own natural interests.

During the Middle Ages, just as the political theory maintained that while a king ruled by divine right, this right gave him no authority to govern wrong, so the social theory held that while a man had a right to private property he had no right to use it against society, nor could the labourer use his own rights to the injury of the same institution. Power, property and labour must be used as a ***function***, i.e., "an activity which embodies and expresses the idea of social purpose." Unless I am mistaken, this is at the basis of our "common law."

As Mediaevalism gave place to the Renaissance this Christian idea was abandoned, and increasingly the obligation was severed from the right, which so became that odious thing, privilege. Intolerable in its injustice and oppression, this privilege, which by the middle of the eighteenth century had become the attribute of the aristocracy, was completely overthrown, in France first of all, and a new doctrine of rights was enunciated and put in operation. Unfortunately the result was in essence simply a transforming of privilege from one body to another, for the old conception of social purpose, as the necessary concomitant of acknowledged rights, did not emerge from the shadows of the Middle Ages; it had been too long forgotten. The new "rights" were exclusively individualistic, in practice, though in the minds of the idealists who formulated them, they had their social aspect. Their promulgation synchronized with the sudden rise and violent expansion of industrialism, and as one country after another followed the lead of England in accepting the new system, they hardened into an iron-clad scheme for the defence of property and the free action of the holders and manipulators of property. Backed by the economic philosophy of Locke, Adam Smith, Bentham and the Manchester School, generally, and the evolutionary theories of the exponents of Darwinism, and abetted by an endless series of statutes, the idea of the exemption of property holders from any responsibility to society for the use of their property, became a fixed part of the mental equipment of modernism. Precisely the same thing happened politically and socially. Rights were personal and implied no necessary obligation to society as a whole; they were personal attributes and as such to be defended at all costs.

Now the result of this profound error as to the existence, nature and limitation of these personal rights has meant simply the destruction of a righteous and unified society which works by cooeperation and fellowship, and the substitution of individuals and corporate bodies who work by competition, strife and mutual aggression towards the attainment of all they can get under the impulse of what was once praised as "enlightened self interest." In other words--war. The conflict that began in 1914 was not a war hurled into the midst of a white peace, it was only a military war arising in the centre of a far greater social war, for there is no other word that is descriptive. Rights that are not contingent on the due discharge of duties and obligations are but hateful privilege; privilege has issue in selfishness and egotism, which in turn work themselves out in warfare and in the hatred that both precedes and follows conflict.

The net result of a century and a half of industrialism is avarice, warfare and hate. Society can continue even when avariciousness is rampant--for a time--and warfare of one sort or another seems inseparable from humanity, at all events it has always been so, but hatred is another matter, for it is the negation of social life and is its solvent. Anger passes; it is sometimes even righteous, but hatred is synonymous with death in that it dissolves every unit, reducing it to its component parts and subjecting each of these to dissolution in its turn. Righteous anger roused the nations into the war that hate had engendered, but hate has followed after and for the moment is victorious. Russia seethes with hatred and is perishing of its poison, while there is not another country in Europe, of those that were involved in the war, where the same is not true in varying degrees; hatred of race for race, of nation for nation, of class for class, of one social or industrial or economic or political institution for another. This, above all else, is the disintegrating influence, and against it no social organism, no civilization can stand. Unless it is abrogated it means an ending of another epoch of human life, a period of darkness and another beginning, some time after the poison has been worked out by misery, adversity and forced repentance.

It is this prevalence of hatred, reinforced by avarice and perpetuated by incessant warfare, that negatives all the efforts that are made towards effecting a correspondence between the divided interests that are the concomitant of industrialism. Strikes and lockouts, trades unions and employers' associations as they are now constituted and as they now operate, syndicalism and Bolshevism and proletarian dictatorships, protective tariffs and commercial spheres of influence, propaganda and subsidized newspapers are all energized by the principle of hate, and no good thing can come of any of them. Nor is it enough to work for the re-establishment of justice even by those methods of righteousness, and with the impulse towards righteousness, which are so different from those which are functioning at present along the lines of contemporary industrial "reform." Justice is a "natural" virtue with a real place in society, but the only saving force today is a supernatural virtue. This, amongst other things, Christ brought into the world and left as the saving force amongst the race He had redeemed and in the society reconstituted in accordance with His will. This supernatural virtue is Charity, sometimes expressed in the simpler form of Love, the essence of the social code of Christianity and the symbol of the New Dispensation as justice was the symbol of the Old. Just in so far as a man or a cult or an interest or a corporation or a state or a generation or a race, relinquishes charity as its controlling spirit, in so far it relinquishes its place in Christian society and its claim to the Christian name, while it is voided of all power for good or possibility of continuance. Where charity is gone, intellectual capacity, effectual power, and even justice itself become, not energies of good, but potent contributions to evil. Is this supernatural gift of charity a mark of contemporary civilization? Does it manifest itself with power today in the dealings between class and class, between interest and interest, between nation and nation? If not, then we have forfeited the name of Christian and betrayed Christian civilization into the hands of its enemies, while our efforts towards saving what is left to us of a once consistent and righteous society will be without result except as an acceleration of the now headlong process of dissolution.

I am not charging any class or any interest or any people with exclusive apostacy. In the end there is little to choose between one or another. Labour is not more culpable than capital, nor the proletarian than the industrial magnate and the financier, nor the nominal secularist than the nominal religionist. Nor am I charging conscious and willful acceptance of wrong in the place of right. It is the institution itself, industrialism as it has come to be, with all its concomitants and derivatives, that has betrayed man to his disgrace and his society to condemnation, and so long as this system endures so long will recovery be impossible and regeneration a vain thing vainly imagined. Charity, that is to say, fellowship, generosity, pity, self-sacrifice, chivalry, all that is comprehended in the thing that Christ was, and preached, and promulgated as the fundamental law of life, cannot come back to the world so long as avarice, warfare and hate continue to exist, and through Charity alone can we find the solution of the industrial and economic problem that ***must*** be solved under penalty of social death.

V
THE POLITICAL ORGANIZATION OF SOCIETY

In these essays, which look towards a new social synthesis, I find myself involved in somewhat artificial subdivisions. Industrial, social and political forces all react one upon another, and the complete social product is the result of the interplay of these forces, cooerdinated and vitalized by philosophy, education and religion. To isolate each factor and consider it separately is apt to result in false values, but there seems no other way in which the subject, which is essentially one, may be divided into the definite parts which are consequent on the form of a course of lectures. In considering now the political estate of the human social organism it will be evident that I hold that this must be contingent on many elements that reveal themselves in a contributory industrial system, in the principles that are embodied in social relationships, and in the general scheme of such a working philosophy of life as may predominate amongst the component parts of the synthetic society which is the product of all these varied energies and the organic forms through which they operate.

Political organization has always been a powerful preoccupation of mankind, and the earliest records testify to its antiquity. The regulation of human intercourse, the delimiting of rights and privileges, protection of life and property, the codifying of laws, vague, various and conflicting, the making of new laws and the enforcing of those that have taken organic form; all these and an hundred other governmental functions, appeal strongly to the mind and touch closely on personal interests. It is no wonder that the political history of human society is the most varied, voluminous and popular in its appeal. At the present moment this problem has, in general, an even more poignant appeal, and no rival except the industrial problem, for in both cases systems that, up to ten years ago, were questioned only by a minority (large in the case of industry, small and obscure in the case of government) have since completely broken down, and it is probable that a political system which had existed throughout the greater part of Europe and the Americas for a century and a half, almost without serious criticism, has now as many assailants as industrialism itself.

The change is startling from the "Triumphant Democracy" period, a space of time as clearly defined and as significant in its characteristics as the "Victorian Era." Before the war, during the war, and throughout the earlier years of the even more devastating "peace," the system which followed the ruin of the Renaissance autocracies, the essential elements in which were an ever-widening suffrage, parliamentary government, and the universal operation of the quantitative standard of values, was never questioned or criticised, except in matters of detail. That it was the most perfect governmental scheme ever devised and that it must continue forever, was held to be axiomatic, and with few exceptions the remedy proposed for such faults as could not possibly escape detection was a still further extension of the democratic principle. Even the war itself was held to be "a war to make the world safe for democracy." It is significant that the form in which this saying now frequently appears is one in which the word "from" is substituted in place of the word "for." It is useless to blink the fact that there is now a distrust of parliamentary and representative government which is almost universal and this distrust, which is becoming widespread, reaches from the Bolshevism of Russia on the one hand, through many intermediate social and intellectual stages, to the conservative elements in England and the United States, and the fast-strengthening royalist "bloc" in France.

In many unexpected places there is visible a profound sense that something is so fundamentally wrong that palliatives are useless and some drastic reform is necessary, a reform that may almost amount to revolution. Lord Bryce still believes in democracy in spite of his keen realizations of its grievous defects, because, as he says, hope is an inextinguishable quality of the human soul. Mr. Chesterton preaches democracy in principle while condemning its mechanism and its workings with his accustomed vigour; the Adamses renounce democracy and all its works while offering no hint as to what could consistently take its place with any better chance of success, while the royalists excoriate it in unmeasured terms and preach an explicit return to monarchy. Meanwhile international Bolshevism, hating the thing as violently as do kings in exile, substitutes a crude and venal autocracy, while organized labour, as a whole, works for the day when a "class-conscious proletariat" will have taken matters into its own hands and established a new aristocracy of privilege in which the present working classes will hold the whip-hand. Meanwhile the more educated element of the general public withdraws itself more and more from political affairs, going its own way and making the best of a bad job it thinks itself taught by experience it cannot mend.

It is useless to deny that government, in the character of its personnel, the quality of its output, the standard of its service and the degree of its beneficence has been steadily deteriorating during the last century and has now reached, in nearly every civilized country, a deplorably low level. Popular representatives are less and less men of character and ability; legislation is absurd in quantity, short-sighted, frivolous, inquisitorial, and in a large measure prompted by selfish interests; administration is reckless, wasteful and inefficient, while it is overloaded in numbers, without any particular aptitude on the part of its members, and in a measure controlled by personal or corporate interests. The whole system is in bad odour for it is shot through and through with the greed for money and influence, while the cynicism of the professional politician and the low average of character, intelligence and manners of the strata of society that increasingly are usurping all power, work towards producing that general contempt and aversion that have become so evident of late and that are a menace to society no less than that of the decaying institution itself.

Confronted by a situation such as this, the natural tendency of those who suffer under it, either in their material interests or their ideals, is to condemn the mechanism, perhaps even the very principles for the operation of which the various machines were devised. Some reject the whole scheme of representative, parliamentary government, and, failing any plausible substitute, are driven back on some form of the soviet, or even government by industrial groups. Those that go to the limit and reject the whole scheme of democracy are in still worse plight for they have no alternative to offer except a restored monarchy, and this, the ***terminus ad quem*** of their logic, their courage will not permit them to avow.

It is a dilemma, but forced, I believe, by the fatal passion of the man of modernism for the machine, the mechanical device, the material equivalent for a thing that has no equivalent, and that is the personal character of the constituents of society and the working factors in a political organism. There was never a more foolish saying than that which is so frequently and so boastfully used: "a government of laws and not of men." This is the exact reversal of what should be recognized as a self-evident truth, viz, that the quality of the men, not the nature of the laws or of the administrative machine, is the determining factor in government. You may take any form of government ever devised by man, monarchy, aristocracy, republic, democracy, yes, or soviet, and if the community in which this government operates has a working majority of men of character, intelligence and spiritual energy, it will be a good government, whereas if the working majority is deficient in these characteristics, or if it makes itself negligible by abstention from public affairs it will be a bad government. There is no one political system which is right while all others are wrong. The monarchy of St. Louis was better than the Third Republic, as this is better than was the monarchy of Louis XV. The aristocracy of Washington was better than the democracy of this year of grace, as this in itself is better than the late junker aristocracy of Prussia. You cannot substitute a machine in place of character, you cannot supersede life by a theory.

This does not mean that the form of government is of no moment, it is of the utmost importance for I cannot too often insist that the organic life of society is the resultant of two forces; spiritual energy working through and upon the material forms towards their improvement or--when this energy is weak or distorted--their degeneration; the material forms acting as a stimulus towards the development of spiritual energy through association and environment that are favourable, or towards its weakening and distortion when these are deterrents because of their own degraded or degrading nature. If it is futile to look for salvation through the mechanism, it is equally futile to try to act directly and exclusively on the character of the social constituents in the patient hope that their defects may be remedied, and the preponderance of character of high value achieved, before catastrophe overtakes the experiment. Life is as sacramental as the Christian religion and Christian philosophy; neither the spiritual substance nor the material accidents can operate alone but only in a conjunction so intimate that it is to all intents and purposes--that is, for the interests and purposes of God in human life--a perfect unity. However completely and even passionately we may realize the determining factor of spiritual energy as this manifests itself through personal character, however deeply we may distrust the machine, we are bound to recognize the paramount necessity of the active interplay of both within the limits of life as we know it on the earth, and therefore it is very much our concern that the machine, whether it is industrial, political, educational, ecclesiastical or social, is as perfect in its nature and stimulating in its operations as we are able to compass.

In the present liquidation of values, theories and institutions we are bound therefore to scrutinize each operating agency of human society, to see wherein it has failed and how it can be bettered, and the problem before us now is the political organism.

Now it appears that in the past there have been just two methods whereby a civil polity has come into existence and established itself for a short period or a long. These two methods are, first, unpremeditated and sometimes unconscious growth; second, calculated and self-conscious revolution. The first method has produced communities, states and empires that frequently worked well and lasted for long periods; the second has had issue in nothing that has endured for any length of time or has left a record of beneficence. Evolution in government is in accord with the processes of life, even to the extent that it is always after a time followed by degeneration; revolution in government is the throwing of a monkey-wrench into the machinery by a disaffected workman, with the wrecking of the machine, the violent stoppage of the works, and frequently the sudden death of the worker as a consequence. The English monarchy from Duke William to Henry VIII, is a case of normal growth by minor changes and modifications, but its subsequent history has been one of revolutions, six or seven having occurred in the last four hundred years; the scheme which now holds, though precariously, is the result of the great democratic revolution accomplished during the reign of Queen Victoria. The free monarchies of Europe which began to take form during the long period of the Dark Ages and pursued their admirable course well through the Middle Ages, were also normal and slow growths; but the revolutions that have followed the Great War will meet a different fate, several of them, indeed, have counted their existence in months and have already passed into history.

If we are wise we shall discount revolutions for the future, for nothing but ill is accomplished by denying life and exalting the ingenious substitutes of ambitious and presumptuous Frankensteins; the result is too often a monster that works cleverly at first, and with a semblance of human intelligence, but in the end shows itself as a destroyer. Our task is to envisage, as clearly as possible, the political systems established amongst us, note their weaknesses either in themselves or in their relationship to society as it is, and then try to find those remedies that can be applied without any violent methods of dislocation or substitution; always bearing in mind the fact that the energizing force that will make them live, preserve them from deterioration, and adapt them to conditions which will ever change, is the spiritual force of human personality, and that this force comes only through the character qualities of the individual components of society.

Now in considering our own case in this day and generation there are first of all two matters to be borne in mind. One is that we shall do well to confine our inquiry to the United States, for while the defects we shall have to point out are common to practically all the contemporary governments of Europe and the Americas, our own enginery is different in certain ways, and our troubles are also different between one example and another. After all, our immediate interest must lie with our own national problems. The other point is that in criticising the workings of government in America we are not necessarily criticising its founders or the creators of its original constitutions, charters, and other mechanisms. The Constitution of the United States, for example, was conceived to meet one series of perfectly definite conditions that have now been superseded by others which are radically, and even diametrically different. The original Constitution was a most able instrument of organic law, but just because it did fit so perfectly conditions as they were four generations ago, it applies but indifferently to present circumstances, and even less well than the Founders hoped would be the case; for the reason that the amendments which were provided for have seldom taken cognizance of these changing conditions, and even when this was done the amendments themselves have not been wisely drawn, while certain of them have been actually disastrous in their nature, others frivolous, and yet more the result of ephemeral and hysterical ebullitions of an engineered public opinion. The same may be said of state constitutions and municipal charters, which have suffered incessant changes, mostly unfortunate and ill-judged, except during the last few years, when a spirit of real wisdom and constructiveness has shown itself, though sporadically and as yet with some timidity.

The reforms, such as they are, are largely in the line of palliatives; the deep-lying factors, those that control both success and failure, are seldom touched upon. The necessary courage--or perhaps temerity--is lacking. What is needed is such a clear seeing of conditions, and such an approach, as manifested themselves in the Constitutional Convention of the United States, for in spite of the many compromises that were in the end necessary to placate a public opinion not untouched by prejudice, superstition and selfishness, the great document--and even more the records of the debates--still brilliantly set forth both the clear-seeing and the lofty attitude that characterized the Convention. Had these men been gathered together today, even the same men, they would frame a very different document, for they took conditions and men as they were, and, with an indestructible hope to glorify their common sense, they produced a masterpiece. It is in the same spirit that we must approach our problem of today.

Now in considering the situation that confronts us, we find certain respects in which either the methods are bad, or the results, or both. There is no unanimity in this criticism, indeed I doubt if any two of us would agree on all the items in the indictment, though we all might unite on one or two. I can only give my own list for what it is worth. In the first place we, in common with all the nations, have drifted into imperialism of a gross scale and illiberal, even tyrannical working. We could hardly do otherwise for such has been the universal tendency for more than an hundred years. By constant progression municipal governments have absorbed into themselves matters that in decency, and with any regard for liberty, belong to the individual. Simultaneously our state governments have followed the same course, infringing even on the just prerogatives of the towns and cities, while, more than all, the national government has robbed the states, the cities and the citizens of what should belong to them, until at last we have an imperial, autocratic, inquisitorial, and largely irresponsible government at Washington that is the one supreme political fact; we are no longer a Federal Republic but an Imperialism, in which is centralized all the authority inherent in the one hundred and ten millions of our population and from which a constantly diminishing stream of what is practically devolved authority, trickles down through state and city to the individual in the last instance--if it gets there at all! This I believe to be absolutely and fatally wrong. In the first place, human society cannot function at this abnormal scale, it is outside the human scale, for in spite of our pride and insolence there are limits on every hand to what man can do. In the second place, I conceive it to be absolutely at variance with any principle of republicanism or democracy or even of free monarchy. It is at one only with the imperialism of Egypt, Babylon, Rome and the late Empire of Germany. In a free monarchy, a republic, or a democracy, the pyramid of political organism stands, not on its point but broad-based and four-square, tapering upward to its final apex. A sane and wholesome society begins with the family--natural or artificial--which has original jurisdiction over a far greater series of rights and privileges than it now commands. From the family certain powers are delegated to the next higher social unit, the village or communal group, which in its turn concedes certain of its inherent rights to the organic group of communities, or states, and finally the states commit to the last and general authority, the national government, some of the elements of authority that have been delegated to them. The principle of this delegation from one organism to another, is common interest and welfare; only those functions which can be performed with more even justice and with greater effectiveness, by the community for example, than by the family, are so delegated. In the same way the several groups commit to their common government only so much as they cannot perform with due justice and equity to the others in the same group. In the end the national government exists only that it may provide for a limited number of national necessities, as for example, defence against extra-national aggression, the conduct of diplomatic relations with foreign powers, the maintaining of a national currency and a national postal service, the provision of courts of last resort, and the raising of revenue for the support of these few and explicit functions.

The first step, it seems to me, towards governmental reform, is decentralization, with a return to the States, the civic communities and the individual citizens of nine-tenths of the powers and the prerogatives that have been taken from them in defiance of abstract justice, of the principles of free government and of the theory of the workable unit of human scale. In a word we must abandon imperialism and all its works and go back to the Federal Republic.

The second cause of our troubles lies, I believe, in the institution of universal suffrage founded on the theory (or dogma) that the electoral franchise is an inalienable right. This doctrine is of recent invention, only coming into force during the "reconstruction period" following the War between the States, when it was brought forward by certain leaders of the Republican party to justify their enfranchisement of the negroes in the hope that by this act they could fix their party in power to perpetuity. In any case, the plan itself has worked badly, both for the community and for many of the voters. It is of course impossible for me to argue the case in detail; I can do hardly more than state my own personal belief, and this is that the question is wholly one of expediency, and that the question of abstract justice and the rights of man does not enter into the consideration. I submit that the electoral franchise should again be accepted as a privilege involving a duty, and not as a right inherent in every adult person of twenty-one years or over and not lunatic or in jail. This privilege, which in itself should confer honour, should be granted to those who demonstrate their capacity to use it honestly and intelligently, and taken away for cause.

The acute critic will not be slow to remind me that this proposition is somewhat beside the case and that it possesses but an academic interest, since we are dealing with a ***fait accompli.*** This is of course perfectly true. The electoral franchise could be so restricted only by the suffrages of the present electorate, and it is inconceivable that any large number, and far less, a majority, of voters would even consider the proposition for a moment. For good or ill we have unrestricted adult suffrage, and there is not the faintest chance of any other basis being established by constitutional means. Something however can be done, and this is a thing of great value and importance. What I suggest is concerted effort towards a measured purification of the electorate through the penalizing of law-breakers by temporary disfranchisement. It is hardly too much to assume that a man who deliberately breaks the law is constructively unfit to vote or to hold office, at all events, conviction for any crime or misdemeanour gives a reasonable ground for depriving the offender of these privileges, at least for a time. The law-breaking element, whether it is millionaire or proletarian, is one of the dangerous factors in society, which would lose nothing if from time to time these gentry were removed from active participation in public affairs. If, for example, any one convicted of minor offenses punishable by fine or imprisonment were disfranchised for a year, if of major offenses, for varying and increasing periods, from five years upwards, and if a second offense during the period of disfranchisement worked an automatic doubling of the time prescribed for a first offense, I conceive that the electorate would be measurably purified and that regard for the law would be stimulated. In one instance I am persuaded that disfranchisement should be for life, and that is in the case of giving or accepting a bribe or otherwise committing a crime against the ballot; this, together with treason against the state, should be sufficient cause for eliminating the offender from all further participation in public affairs. If the electorate could be purified after this fashion, and if more stringent laws could be passed in the matter of naturalization of aliens, together with iron-clad requirements that every voter should be able to speak, read and write the English language, we should have achieved something towards the safeguarding of the suffrage.

The third weakness in our system, and in some respect the most dangerous, as it is in all respects the most pestiferous, is the insanity of law-making. All parliamentary governments suffer from this malady, but that of the United States most grievously, and this is true of the national government, the states and the municipalities. It has become the conviction of legislative bodies that they must justify their existence by making laws, and the more laws they pass the better they have discharged their duties. The thing has become a scandal and an oppression, for the liberties of American citizens and the just prerogatives of the states and the cities, as vital human groups, have been more infringed upon, reduced, and degraded by free legislation than ever happened in similar communities by the action of absolute monarchs. It is a folly that works its insidious injury in two ways; first by confusing life by innumerable laws ill-advised, ill-drawn, mutually contradictory, ephemeral in their nature, inquisitorial in their workings; second, by creating a condition where any personal or factious interest can be served by due process of law, until at last we have reached a point where liberty itself has largely ceased to exist and we find ourselves crushed under a tyranny of popular government no less oppressive than the tyranny of absolutism. Nor is this all; the mania for making laws has bred a complete and ingenious and singularly effective system of getting laws made by methods familiar to the members of all legislative bodies whether they are city councils, state legislatures or the national congress, and this means opportunities for corruption, and methods of corruption, that are fast degrading government in the United States to a point where there is none so poor as to do it reverence. The whole system is preposterous and absurd, breeding not only bad laws, but a widespread contempt of law, while the personal freedom for which democracy once fought, is fast becoming a memory.

The trouble began as a result of one of the elements in the American Constitution which was the product not of the sound common sense and the lofty judgment of the framers, but of a weak yielding to one of the doctrinaire fads of the time that had no relationship to life but was the invention of political theorists, and that was the unnatural separation of the executive, legislative and judicial functions of government. The error has worked far and the superstition still holds. What is needed is an initiative in legislation, centred in one responsible head or group, that, while functioning in all normal and necessary legislative directions, still allows individual initiative on the part of the legislators, as a supplementary, or corrective, or protective agency. No government functions well in fiscal matters without a budget: what we need in legislative matters is a legislative budget, and by this phrase, I mean that the primary agency for the proposing of laws should be the chief executive of a city, or state or the nation, with the advice and consent of his heads of departments who would form his cabinet or council.

Under this plan the Governor and Council, for example, would at the opening of each legislative session present a programme or agenda of such laws as they believed the conditions to demand, and in the shape of bills accurately drawn by the proper law officer of the government. No such "government" bill could be referred to committee but must be discussed in open session, and until the bills so offered had been passed or refused, no private bill could be introduced. A procedure such as this would certainly reduce the flood of private bills to reasonable dimensions while it would insure a degree of responsibility now utterly lacking. There is now no way in which the author of a foolish or dangerous bill which has been enacted into law by a majority of the legislature, can be held to account and due responsibility imposed upon him, but the case would be very different if a mayor, a governor or the President of the United States made himself responsible for a law or a series of laws, by offering them for action in his own name. Certainly if this method were followed we should be preserved in great measure from the hasty, confused and frivolous legislation that at present makes up the major part of the output of our various legislative bodies. One of the greatest gains would be the reduction of the annual grist to a size where each act could be considered and debated at sufficient length to guarantee as reasonable a conclusion as would be possible to the members of the legislative body. The deplorable device of instituting committees, to each of which certain bunches of bills are referred before they are permitted to come before the house, would be no longer necessary. This system, which became necessary in order to deal with the enormous mass of undigested matter which has overwhelmed every legislature as a result of the present chaotic and irresponsible procedure, is perhaps both the most undemocratic device ever put in practice by a democracy, and the most fruitful of venality, corruption and injustice. It is unnecessary to labour this point for everyone knows its grave evils, but there seems no way to get rid of it unless some curb is placed on the number of bills introduced in any session. The British Parliament is not necessarily a model of intelligent or capable procedure, but where in one session at Westminster no more than four hundred bills were introduced, at Washington, for the same period, the count ran well over twelve thousand! Manifestly some committee system is inevitable under conditions such as this, but under the committee system free government and honest legislation are difficult of attainment.

One would not of course prevent the proposal of a bill by any member of the legislature, indeed this free action would be absolutely necessary as a measure of protection against executive oppression, but this should be prohibited until after the government programme had been disposed of. After that task was accomplished the legislature might sit indefinitely, or as long as the public would stand it, for the purpose of considering private bills, and these could be referred to committees as at present. The chances are, however, that the government programme would cover the most essential matters and what would remain would be the edifying spectacle of Solons solemnly considering such questions as the minimum length of sheets on hotel beds, the limitation in inches and fractions, of the heels of women's shoes, the amount of flesh that could be legally exposed by a bathing suit, or the pensioning of a Swedish Assistant Janitor,--all of which are the substance of actual bills introduced in various State legislatures during the session last closed.

Another grave weakness in our system is the election by popular vote of many judicial and administrative officers, coupled with the vigorous remnants of the old and degrading "spoils system" whereby many thousands of strictly non-political offices are almost automatically vacated after any partisan victory. I cannot trust myself to speak of the infamy of an elective judiciary; fortunately I live in a state where this worst abuse of democratic practice does not exist, and so it touches me only in so far as it offends the sense of decency and justice. In the other cases it is only a question of efficient and intelligent administration. There is an argument for electing the chief executive of a city, a state or the nation, by popular vote, and the same holds in the case of the lower house of the legislature where a bi-cameral system exists, but there is no argument for the popular election of the administrative officers of a state. There is even less,--if there can be less than nothing--for the changes in personnel that take place after every election. Civil service reform has done a world of good, but as yet it has not gone far enough in some directions, while its mechanism of examinations is defective in principle in that it leaves out the personal equation and establishes its tests only along a very few of the many lines that actually exist. I would offer it as a proposition that no election should in itself affect the status of any man except the man elected, and, in the case of a mayor or governor or the President, those who are directly responsible to him and to his administration for carrying out his policies; and further, that the voter, when he votes, should vote once and for one man in his city, once and for one man in his state, and once and for one man in the nation, and that man, in each case, should be his representative in the lower branch of the legislative body. Choosing administrative officials by majority vote, and the election of judges for short terms by the same method, are absurdities of a system fast falling into chaos. The maintenance of a bi-cameral legislative organization, with the choosing of the members of both houses by the same electorate is in the same class, a perfectly irrational anomaly which violates the first principles of logic and leads only to legislative incompetence, and worse. The referendum is of precisely the same nature, but this already has become a ***reductio ad absurdum,*** and can hardly survive the discredit into which it has fallen. In any reorganization of government looking towards better results, these elements must disappear.

As a matter of fact, government has come to occupy altogether too large a place in our consciousness; naturally, for it has come to a point where it pursues us--and overtakes us--at every turn. Democracies always govern too much, that is one of their great weaknesses. Elections, law-making, and getting and holding office, have become an obsession and they shadow our days. So insistent and incessant are the demands, so artificial and unreal the issues, so barren of vital results all this pandemonium of partisanship and change, the more intelligent and scrupulous are losing interest in the whole affair, and while they increasingly withdraw to matters of a greater degree of reality those who subsist on the proceeds gain the power, and hold it. At the very moment when the women of the United States have been given the vote, there are many men (and women also) who begin to think that the vote is a very empty institution and in itself practically void of power to effect anything of really vital moment. I am not now defending this position, I only assert that it exists, and I believe it is due to the degradation of government through the very modifications and transformations that have been effected, since the time of Andrew Jackson, in a perfectly honest attempt at improvement.

The best government is that which does the least, which leaves local matters in the hands of localities, and personal matters in the hands of persons, and which is modestly inconspicuous. Good government establishes, or recognizes, conditions which are stable, reliable, and that may be counted on for more than two years, or four years, at a time. It has continuity, it preserves tradition, and it follows custom and common law. Such a government is neither hectic in its vicissitudes nor inquisitorial in its enactments. It is cautious in its expenditures, efficient in its administration, proud in maintaining its standards of honour, justice and "noblesse oblige." Good government is august and handsome; it surrounds itself with dignity and ceremony, even at times with splendour and pageantry, for these things are signs of self-respect and the outward showing of high ideals--or may be made so; that is what good manners and ceremony and beauty are for. Finally, good government is where the laws of Christian morals and courtesy and charity that are supposed to hold between Christian men hold equally, even more forcefully, in public relations both domestic and foreign. Where government of this nature exists, whether the form is monarchical, republican or democratic, there is liberty; where these conditions do not obtain the form matters not at all, for there is a servile state.

At the risk of being tedious I will try to sketch the rough outlines of what, in substance, I believe to be that form of civil polity which, based on what now exists, changes only along lines that would perhaps tend towards establishing and maintaining those ideals of liberty, order and justice which have always been the common aim of those who have striven to reform a condition of things where they were attained indifferently or not at all.

The primary and effective social and political unit is the "vill" or commune; that is to say, a group of families and individuals living in one neighbourhood, and of a size that would permit all the members to know one another if they wished to do so, and also the coming together of all those holding the electoral franchise, for common discussion and action. The average American country town, uninvaded by industrialism, is the natural type, for here the "town meeting" of our forefathers is practicable, and this remains the everlasting frame and model of self-government. In the case of a city the primary unit would be of approximately the same size, and the entire municipality would be divided into wards each containing, say, about five hundred voters. These primary units would possess a real unity and a very large measure of autonomy, but they would be federated for certain common purposes which would vary in number and importance in proportion to the closeness of their common interests, from the county, made up of a number of small villages, to the city which would comprise as many wards as might be numerically necessary, and whose central government would administer a great many more affairs than would the county. The city would be in effect a federation of the wards or boroughs.

The individual voter would exercise his electoral franchise and perform his political duties only within the primary unit (the township or ward) where he had legal residence. At an annual "town meeting" he would vote for the "selectmen" or the ward council who would have in charge the local interests of the primary unit, which would be comprehensive in the case of a township, necessarily more limited in the case of a ward. These local boards would elect their own chairmen who would also form the legislative body of the county or the municipality. At the same town meeting the voter would cast his ballot for a representative in the lower legislative body of the state. In the smaller commonwealths each township or ward would elect its own representative, but in states of excessive population representation would have to be on the basis of counties and municipalities, for no legislative body should contain more than a very few hundred members. Nominations in the town meeting should be *viva voce,* elections by secret ballot. Legislation should be primarily on the initiative of the selectmen or ward council, and voting should be *viva voce.* With the exercise of his privilege of speaking and voting at the meetings of his primary unit, the direct political action of the citizen would cease.

The secondary unit would be the county or the city. Here the legislative body would consist of the presiding officers of the township or ward governments. The sheriff of a county or the mayor of a city would be chosen by these legislative bodies from their own number and should hold office for a term of several years, while the local governments, and therefore the legislative bodies of the county or the city, would be chosen annually. The chief executive of a county or city would appoint all heads of departments who would form his advisory council, and he would also frame and submit annually both a fiscal and a legislative budget.

The tertiary unit is the state, which is a federation of the counties and cities forming some one of the historic divisions of the United States. The legislature would as now be composed of two chambers, one made up of representatives of the primary units, holding office for a brief term, and a second representing the secondary units and chosen by their governing bodies for a long term. The logic of a bi-cameral system demands that the lower house should represent the changing will of the people, the upper, in so far as possible, its cumulative wisdom and the continuity of tradition, while, as already stated, the whole principle is vitiated if both houses are chosen by the same electorate. The chief executive should be chosen by the legislative chambers in joint session, from a panel made up of their own membership and the heads of the county and city governments. He should hold office for a long term, preferably for an indeterminate period contingent on "good behaviour." In this case his cabinet, or council of the heads of departments, would of course be responsible to the legislature and would resign on a formal vote of censure or "lack of confidence." The Governor would have the same power of appointment, and the same authority to present fiscal and legislative budgets as, already specified in the case of a mayor of a city. No "commissions," unpaid or otherwise, should be permitted, all the administrative functions of government being performed by the various departments and their subordinate bureaux.

The national government is the final social and political unit, though it is conceivable that with a territory and population as great and diversified as that of the United States, and bearing in mind the great discrepancy in size between the states, something might be gained by the institution of a system of provinces, some five or six in all, made up of states grouped in accordance with their general community of interests, as for example, all New England, New York, Pennsylvania, New Jersey and Delaware; the states of the old Confederacy, those of the Pacific Coast, and so on. The point need not be pressed here, but there are considerations in its favour. In any case the nation as a whole is the final federal unit. Here the lower legislative house would consist of not more than four hundred members, allocated on a basis of population and elected by the representative bodies of the primary units (the townships and city wards) as already described. The members of the upper house would be elected by the legislative bodies of the several states on nomination by the Governor. The chief executive of the nation would be chosen by the two legislative bodies, in joint session, from amongst the then governors of the several states. He should certainly hold office for "good behaviour," and his cabinet would be responsible to the legislature as provided for in the case of the state governments.

I do not offer this programme with any pride of paternity; probably it would not work very well, but it could hardly prove less efficacious than our present system under conditions as they have come to be. This cannot continue indefinitely, for it is so hopelessly defective that it is bound to bring about its own ruin, with the probable substitution of some doctrinaire device engendered by the natural revolt against an intolerable abuse. If only we could see conditions clearly and estimate them at something approaching their real value, we should rapidly develop a constructive public opinion that, even though it represented a minority, might by the very force behind it compel the majority to acquiesce in a radical reformation. Unfortunately we do not do this, we are hypnotized by phrases and deluded by vain theories, as Mr. Chesterton says:

"So drugged and deadened is the public mind by the conventional public utterances, so accustomed have we grown to public men talking this sort of pompous nonsense and no other, that we are sometimes quite shocked by the revelation of what men really think, or else of what they really say."

We do, now and then, confess that legislation is as a whole foolish, frivolous and opportunist; that administration is wasteful, incompetent and frequently venal; that the governmental personnel, legislative, administrative and executive, is of a low order in point of character, intelligence and culture--and tending lower each day. We admit this, for the evidence is so conspicuous that to deny it would be hypocrisy, but something holds us back from recognizing the nexus between effect and cause. Unrestricted immigration, universal suffrage, rotation in office, the subjection of many offices and measures to popular vote, the parliamentary system, government by political parties--all these customs and habits into which we have fallen have arrived at failure which presages disaster. They have failed because the character of the people that functioned through these various engines had failed, diluted by the low mentality and character-content of millions of immigrants and their offspring, degraded by the false values and vicious standards imposed by industrial civilization, foot-loose from all binding and control of a vital and potent religious impulse or religious organism.

It is the old, vicious circle; spiritual energy declines or is diverted into wrong channels; thereupon the physical forms, social, industrial, political, slip a degree or two lower out of sympathy with the failing energy, and these in their turn exert a degrading influence on the waning spiritual force, which declines still further only to be pulled lower still by the material agencies which continue their progressive declension. Theories, no matter how high-minded and altruistic, cannot stand before a condition such as this, for self-protection decrees otherwise even if the higher motive of doing right things and getting right things just because they *are* right, does not come into effective operation. The evil results of the institutions I have catalogued above are not to be denied, and the institutions themselves must be reformed or altogether abandoned, in the face of the loud-mouthed exhortations of those who now make them their means of livelihood, and even at the expense of the honest upholders of theories and doctrines that do credit to their humanitarianism but have been weighed and found wanting.

I am anxious not to put this plan for the reform, in root and branch, of our political institutions, on the low level of mere caution and self-defense. The motive power of this is fear, and fear is only second to hate in its present position as a controlling force in society. We should have good government not because it is economical and ensures what are known as "good business conditions," and promises a peaceful continuance of society, but because it is as worthy an object of creative endeavour as noble art or a great literature or a just and merciful economic system, or a life that is full of joy and beauty and wholesome labour. The political organism is in a sense the microcosm of life itself, and it should be society lifted up to a level of dignity, majesty and nobility. The doctrine that in a democracy the government must exactly express the numerical preponderance in the social synthesis, and that, if this happens to be ignorant, mannerless and corrupt, then the government must be after the same fashion, is a low and a cowardly doctrine. Government should be better than the majority; better than the minority if this has advantage over the other. It should be of the best that man can compass, resting above him as in some sort an ideal; the visible expression of his better self, and the better self of the society of which he is a part. If a political system, any political system, produces any other result; if it has issue in a representation of the lowest and basest in society, or even of the general average, then it is a bad system and it must be redeemed or it will bring an end that is couched in terms of catastrophe.

Reform is difficult, perhaps even impossible of attainment under the existing system where universal, unlimited suffrage and the party system are firmly intrenched as opponents of vital reform, and where representation and legislation take their indelible colour from these unfortunate institutions. It must freely be admitted that there is no chance of eliminating or recasting either one or the other by the recognized methods of platform support and mass action through the ballot. It comes in the end to a change of viewpoint and of heart on the part of the individual. No party, no political leader would for a moment endorse any one of the principles or methods I have suggested, for this would be a suicidal act. The newspaper, irresponsible, anonymous, directed by its advertizing interests or by those more sinister still, yet for all that the factor that controls the opinions of those who hold the balance of power in the community as it is now constituted, would reject them with derision, while in themselves they are radically opposed to the personal interests of the majority. The only hope of lifting government to the level of dignity and capacity it should hold, lies in the individual. It is necessary that we should see things clearly, estimate conditions as they are, and think through to the end. We do not do this. We admit, in a dull sort of way, that matters are not as they should be, that legislation is generally silly and oppressive, that taxation is excessive, that administration is wasteful and reckless and incompetent, for we know these things by experience. We accept them, however, with our national good-nature and easy tolerance, assuming that they are inseparable from democratic government--as indeed they are, but not for a moment does any large number think of questioning the principle, or even the system, that must take the responsibility. When disgust and indifference reach a certain point we stop voting, that is all. At the last presidential election less than one half the qualified voters took the trouble to cast their ballots, while in Boston (which is no exception) it generally happens that at a municipal elections the ballots cast are less than one-third the total electorate. I wonder how many there are here today who have ever been to a ward meeting, or have sat through a legislative session of a city government, as of Boston for example, or have listened to the debates in a state house of representatives, or analyzed the annual grist of legislative bills, or have sat for an hour or two in the Senate or House at Washington. Such an experience is, I assure you, illuminating, for it shows exactly why popular government is what it is, while it forms an admirable basis for a constructive revision of judgment as to the soundness of accepted principles and the validity of accepted methods.

Our political attitude today is based on an inherited and automatic acceptance of certain perfectly automatic formulae. We neither see things clearly, estimate conditions as they are, nor think a proposition through to the end: we are obsessed by old formulae, partisan "slogans" and newspaper aphorisms; the which is both unworthy and perilous. Let us see things clearly for a moment; if we do this anything is possible, no matter how idealistic and apparently impracticable it may be. Is there any one who would confess that character and intelligence are now a helpless minority in this nation? Such an admission would be almost constructive treason. The instinct of the majority is right, but it is defective in will and it is subservient to base leadership, while its power for good is negatived by the persistence of a mass of formulae that, under radically changed conditions, have ceased to be beneficent, or even true, and have become a clog and a stumbling block.

I may not have indicated better ideals or sounder methods of operation, but the true ideals exist and it is not beyond our ability to discover a better working system. Partisanship cannot reveal either one or the other, nor are they the fruit of organization or the attribute of political leadership. They belong to the common citizen, to you, to the individual, and if once superstition is cast out and we fall back on right reason and the eternal principles of the Christian ethic and the Christian ideal, we shall not find them difficult of attainment; and once attained they can be put in practice, for the ill thing exists only on sufferance, the right thing establishes itself by force of its very quality of right.

VI
THE FUNCTION OF EDUCATION AND ART

When, as on occasion happens, some hostile criticism is leveled against the civilization of modernism, or against some one of its many details, the reply is ready, and the faultfinder is told that the defect, if it exists, will in the end be obviated by the processes of popular education. Pressed for more explicit details as to just what may be the nature of this omnipotent and sovereign "education," the many champions give various answer, depending more or less on the point of view and the peculiar predilections of each, but the general principles are the same. Education, they say, consist of two things; the formal practice and training of the schools, and the experience that comes through the use of certain public rights and privileges, such as the ballot, the holding of office, service on juries, and through various experiences of the practice of life, as the reading of newspapers (and perhaps books), the activities of work, business and the professions, and personal association with other men in social, craft, and professional clubs and other organizations.

With the second category of education through experience we need not deal at this time; it is a question by itself and of no mean quality; the matter I would consider is the more formal and narrow one of scholastic training in so far as it bears on the Great Peace that, though perhaps after many days, must follow the Great War and the little peace.

Answering along this line, the protagonists of salvation through education pretty well agree that the thing itself means the widest possible extension of our public school system, with free state universities and technical schools, and the extension of the educational period, with laws so rigid, and enforcement so pervasive and impartial, that no child between the ages of six and sixteen can possibly escape. This free, compulsory and universal education is assumed to be scrupulously secular and hedged about with every safeguard against the insidious encroachments of religion; it will aim to give a little training in most of the sciences, and much in the practical necessities of business life, as for example, stenography, book-keeping, advertising and business science; it will cover a broad field of manual training leading to "graduate courses" in special technical schools; the "laboratory method" and "field practice" will be increasingly developed and applied; Latin, Greek, logic and ancient history will be minimized or done away with altogether, and modern languages, applied psychology and contemporary history will be correspondingly emphasized. As for the state university, it will allow the widest range of free electives, and as an university it will aim to comprise within itself every possible department of practical activity, such as business administration, journalism, banking and finance, foreign trade, political science, psycho-analysis, mining, sanitary engineering, veterinary surgery, as well as law, medicine, agriculture, and civil and mechanical engineering. I am curious to inquire at this time if education such as this does, as a matter of fact, educate, and how far it my be relied upon as a corrective for present defects in society; or rather, first of all, whether education of this, or of any sort, may be looked on as a sufficient saving force, and whether general education, instead of being extended should not be curtailed, or rather safeguarded and restricted.

I have already tried to indicate, in my lecture on the Social Organism, certain doubts that are now arising as to the prophylactic and regenerative powers of education, whether this is based on the old foundation of the Trivium and Quadrivium under the supreme dominion of Theology, or on the new foundation of utilitarianism and applied science under the dominion of scientific pedagogy. While the active-minded portion of society believed ardently in progressive evolution, in the sufficiency of the intellect, the inerrancy of the scientific method, and the transmission by inheritance of acquired characteristics, this supreme confidence in free, secular, compulsory education as the cure-all of the profuse and pervasive ills of society was not only natural but inevitable. I submit that experience has measurably modified the situation, and that we are bound therefore to reconsider our earlier persuasions in the light of somewhat revealing events.

We may admit that the system of modern education works measurably well so far as intellectual training is concerned; *training* as distinguished from development. It works measurably well also in preparing youth for participation in the life of applied science and for making money in business and finance. Conscientious hard labour has been given, and is being given, to making it more effective along these lines, and almost every year some new scheme is brought forward enthusiastically, tried out painstakingly, and then cast aside ignominiously for some new and even more ingenious device. The amount of education is enormous; the total of money spent on new foundations, courses, buildings, equipment--on everything but the pay of the teachers--is princely; the devotion of the teachers, themselves, in the face of inadequate wages, is exemplary, and yet, somehow the results are disappointing. The truth is, the development of *character* is not in proportion to the development of public and private education. The moral standing of the nation, taken as a whole, has been degenerating; in business, in public affairs, in private life, until the standards of value have been confused, the line of demarcation between right and wrong blurred to indistinctness, and the old motives of honour, duty, service, charity, chivalry and compassion are no longer the controlling motive, or at least the conscious aspiration, of active men.

This is not to say that these do not exist; the period that has seen the retrogression has recorded also a reaction, and there are now perhaps more who are fired by the ardent passion for active righteousness, than for several generations, but the average is lower, for where, many times in the past, there has been a broad, general average of decency, now the disparity is great between the motives that drive society as a whole, and its methods of operation, and the remnant that finds itself an unimportant minority. Newspapers are perhaps hardly a fair criterion of the moral status of a people--or of anything else for that matter--but what they record, and the way they do it, is at least an indication of a condition, and after every possible allowance has been made, what they record is a very alarming standard of public and private morality, both in the happenings themselves and in the fashion of their publicity.

No one would claim that the responsibility for this weakening of moral standards rests predominantly on the shoulders of the educational system of today; the causes lie far deeper than this, but the point I wish to make is that the process has not been arrested by education, in spite of its prevalence, and that therefore it is unwise to continue our exclusive faith in its remedial offices. The faith was never well founded. Education can do much, but what it does, or can do, is to foster and develop ***inherent possibilities,*** whether these are of character, intelligence or aptitude: it cannot put into a boy or man what was not there, ***in posse,*** at birth, and humanly speaking, the diversity of potential in any thousand units is limited only by the number itself. Whether our present educational methods are those best calculated to foster and develop these inherent possibilities, so varied in nature and degree, is the question, and it is a question the answer to which depends largely on whether we look on intelligence, capacity or character as the thing of greatest moment. For those who believe that character is the thing of paramount importance--amongst whom I count myself--the answer must be in the negative.

Nor is an affirmative reply entirely assured when the question is asked as to the results in the case of intellect and capacity. There are few who would claim that in either of these directions the general standard is now as high as it was, for example, in the last half of the last century. The Great War brought to the front few personalities of the first class, and the peace that has followed has an even less distinguished record to date. We may say with truth, I think, that the last ten years have provided greater issues, and smaller men to meet them in the capacity of leaders, than any previous crisis of similar moment. The art of leadership, and the fact of leadership, have been lost, and without leadership any society, particularly a democracy, is in danger of extinction.

Here again one cannot charge education with our lack of men of character, intelligence and capacity to lead; as before, the causes lie far deeper, but the almost fatal absence at this time of the personalities of such force and power that they can captain society in its hours of danger from war or peace, must give us some basis for estimating the efficiency of our educational theory and practice, and again raise doubts as to whether here also we shall be well advised if we rely exclusively upon it as the ultimate saviour of society, while we are bound to ask whether its methods, even of developing intelligence and capacity, are the best that can be devised.

Another point worth considering is this. So long as we could lay the flattering unction to our souls that acquired characteristics were heritable, and that therefore if an outcast from Posen, migrating to America, had taken advantage of his new opportunities and so had developed his character-potential, amassed money and acquired a measure of education and culture, he would automatically transmit something of this to his offspring, who would start so much the further forward and would tend normally to still greater advance, and so on *ad infinitum,* so long we were justified in enforcing the widest measure of education on all and sundry, and in waiting in hope for a future when the cumulative process should have accomplished its perfect work. Now, however, we are told that this hope is vain, that acquired characteristics are not transmitted by heredity, and that the old folk-proverb "it is only three generations between shirtsleeves and shirtsleeves," is perhaps more scientifically exact than the evolutionary dictum of the nineteenth century. Which is what experience and history have been teaching, lo, these many years.

The question then seems to divide itself into three parts; (a) are we justified in pinning our faith in ultimate social salvation to free, secular, and compulsory education carried to the furthest possible limits; (b) if not, then what precisely is the function of formal education; and (c) this being determined, is our present method adequate, and if not how should it be modified?

It is unwise to speak dogmatically along any of these lines, they are too blurred and uncertain. I can only express an individual opinion.

It seems to me that life unvaryingly testifies to the extreme disparity of potential in individuals and in families and in racial strains, though in the two latter the difference is not necessarily absolute and permanent, but variable in point of both time and degree. In individuals the limit of this potentiality is inherent, and it can neither be completely inhibited by adverse education and environment nor measurably extended by favourable education and environment. Characteristics acquired ***outside*** inherent limitations are personal and non-heritable, however intimately they may have become a part of the individual himself.

If this is true, then the question of education becomes personal also; that is to say, we educate for the individual, and with an eye to the part he himself is to play in society. We do not look for cumulative results but in a sense deal with each personality in regard to itself alone. I think this has a bearing both on the extent to which education should be enforced and on the quality and method of education itself, and though the contention will receive little but ridicule, I am bound to say that I hold that ***general*** education should be reduced in quantity and considerably changed in nature.

If the limit of development is substantially determined in each individual and cannot be extended by human agencies (I say "human" because God in His wisdom and by His power can raise up a prophet or a saint out of the lowest depths, and frequently does so), then the quantity and extent of general education should be determined not by a period of years and the facilities offered by a government liberal in its expenditures, but entirely by the demonstrated or indicated capacity of the individual. Our educational system should, so far as it is free and compulsory, normally end with the high school grade. Free college, university and technical training should not be provided, except for those who had given unmistakable evidences that they could, and probably would, use it to advantage. This would be provided for by non-competitive scholarships, limited in number only by the number of capable candidates, and determination of this capacity would be, not on the basis of test examinations, but on an average record covering a considerable period of time. It is doubtful if even these scholarships should be wholly free; some responsibility should be recognized, for a good half of the value of a thing (perhaps all its value) lies in working for it. A grant without service, a favour accepted without obligations, privilege without function, both cheapen and degrade.

Let us now turn to the second question, i.e., what precisely is the function of formal education. For my own part I can answer this in a sentence. It is primarily the fostering and development of the character-potential inherent in each individual. In this process intellectual training and expansion and the furthering of natural aptitude have a part, but this is secondary to the major object which is the development of character.

This is not in accordance with the practice or the theory of recent times, and in this fact lies one of the prime causes of failure. The one thing man exists to accomplish is character; not worldly success and eminence in any line, not the conquest of nature (though some have held otherwise), not even "adaptation to environment" in the ***argot*** of last century science, but ***character;*** the assimilation and fixing in personality of high and noble qualities of thought and deed, the furtherance, in a word, of the eternal sacramental process of redemption of matter through the operation of spiritual forces. Without this, social and political systems, imperial dominion, wealth and power, a favourable balance of trade avail nothing; with it, forms and methods and the enginery of living will look out for themselves. And yet this thing which comprises "the whole duty of man" has, of late, fallen into a singular disregard, while the constructive forces that count have either been discredited and largely abandoned, as in the case of religion, or, like education, turned into other channels or reversed altogether, as has happened with the idea and practice of obedience, discipline, self-denial, duty, honour and unselfishness; surely the most fantastic issue of the era of enlightenment, of liberty and of freedom of conscience.

As a matter of fact character, as the chief end of man and the sole guaranty of a decent society, has been neglected; it was not disregarded by any conscious process, but the headlong events that have followed since the fifteenth century have steadily distorted our judgment and confused our standards of value even to reversal. By an imperceptible process other matters have come to engage our interest and control our action, until at last we are confronted by the nemesis of our own unwisdom, and we entertain the threat of a dissolving civilization just because the forces we have engendered or set loose have not been curbed or directed by that vigorous and potent personal character informing a people and a society, that we had forgot in our haste and that alone could give us safety.

Formal education is but one of the factors that may be employed towards the development of character; you cannot so easily separate one force in life from another, assigning a specific duty here, a definite task there. That is one of the weaknesses of our time, the water-tight compartment plan of high specialization, the cellular theory of efficiency. Life must be seen as a whole, organized as a whole, lived as a whole. Every thought, every emotion, every action, works for the building or the unbuilding of character, and this synthesis of living must be reestablished before we can hope for social regeneration. Nevertheless formal education may be made a powerful factor, even now, and not only in this one specific direction, but through this, for the accomplishing of that unification of life that already is indicated as the next great task that is set before us; and this brings me to a consideration of the last of the questions I have proposed for answer, viz.: is our present system of education adequate to the sufficient development of character, and if not, how should it be modified?

I do not think it adequate, and experience seems to me to prove the point. It has not maintained the sturdy if sometimes acutely unpleasant character of the New England stock, or the strong and handsome character of the race that dwelt in the thirteen original colonies as this manifested itself well into the last century, and it has, in general, bred no new thing in the millions of immigrants and their descendants who have flooded the country since 1840 and from whom the public schools and some of the colleges are largely recruited. It is not a question of expanded brain power or applied aptitude, but of character, and here there is a larger measure of failure than we had a right to expect. And yet, had we this right? The avowed object of formal education is mental and vocational training, and by no stretch of the imagination can we hold these to be synonymous with character. We have dealt with and through one thing alone, and that is the intellect, whereas character is rather the product of emotions judiciously stimulated, balanced (not controlled) by intellect, and applied through active and varied experience. Deliberately have we cut out every emotional and spiritual factor; not only religion and the fine arts, but also the studies, and the methods of study, and the type of text-books, that might have helped in the process of spiritual and emotional development. We have eliminated Latin and Greek, or taught them as a branch of philology; we have made English a technical exercise in analysis and composition, disregarding the moral and spiritual significance of the works of the great masters of English; we minimize ancient history and concentrate on European history since the French Revolution, and on the history of the United States, and because of the sensitiveness of our endless variety of religionists (pro forma) text books are written which leave religion out of history altogether--and frequently economics and politics as well when these cannot be made to square with popular convictions; philosophy and logic are already pretty well discarded, except for special electives and post-graduate courses, and as for art in its multifarious forms we know it not, unless it be in the rudimentary and devitalized form of free-hand drawing and occasional concerted singing. The only thing that is left in the line of emotional stimulus is competitive athletics, and for this reason I sometimes think it one of the most valuable factors in public education. It has, however, another function, and that is the coordination of training and life; it is in a sense an ***ecole d'application,*** and through it the student, for once in a way, tries out his acquired mental equipment and his expanding character--as well as his physical prowess--against the circumstances of active vitality. It is just this sort of thing that for so long made the "public schools" of England, however limited or defective may have been the curriculum, a vital force in the development of British character.

At best, however, this seems to me but an indifferent substitute, an inadequate "extra," doing limitedly the real work of education by indirection. What we need (granting my assumption of character as the *terminus ad quem*) is an educational system so recast that the formal studies and the collateral influences and the school life shall be more coordinated in themselves and with life, and that the resulting stimulus shall be equally operative along intellectual, emotional and creative lines.

It is sufficiently easy to make suggestions as to how this is to be accomplished, to lay out programmes and lay down curricula, but here as elsewhere this does not amount to much; the change must come and the institutions develop as the result of the operations of life. If we can change our view of the object of education, the very force of life, working through experience, will adequately determine the forms. It is not therefore as a meticulous and mechanical system that I make the following suggestions as to certain desirable changes, but rather to indicate more exactly what I mean by a scheme of education that will work primarily towards the development of character.

Now in the first place, I must hold that there can be no education which works primarily for character building, that is not interpenetrated at every point by definite, concrete religion and the practice of religion. As I shall try to show in my last two lectures, religion is the force or factor that links action with life. It is the only power available to man that makes possible a sound standard of comparative values, and with philosophy teaching man how to put things in their right order, it enters to show him how to control them well, while it offers the great constructive energy that makes the world an orderly unity rather than a type of chaos. Until the Reformation there was no question as to this, and even after, in the nations that accepted the great revolution, the point was for a time maintained; thereafter the centrifugal tendency in Protestantism resulted in such a wealth of mutually antagonistic sects that the application of the principle became impracticable, and for this, as well as for more fundamental reasons, it fell into desuetude. The condition is as difficult to-day for the process of denominational fission has gone steadily forward, and as this energy of the religious influence weakens the strenuosity of maintenance strengthens. With our 157 varieties of Protestantism confronting Catholicism, Hebraism, and a mass of frank rationalism and infidelity as large in amount as all others combined, it would seem at first sight impossible to harmonize free public education with concrete religion in any intimate way. So it is; but if the principle is recognized and accepted, ways and means will offer themselves, and ultimately the principle will be embodied in a workable scheme.

For example; there is one thing that can be done anywhere, and whenever enough votes can be assembled to carry through the necessary legislation. At present the law regards with an austere disapproval that reflects a popular opinion (now happily tending towards decay), what are known as "denominational schools" and other institutions of learning. Those that maintain the necessity of an intimate union between religion and education, as for example the great majority of Roman Catholics and an increasing number of Episcopalians and Presbyterians, are taxed for the support of secular public schools which they do not use, while they must maintain at additional, and very great, expense, parochial and other private schools where their children may be taught after a fashion which they hold to be necessary from their own point of view. Again, state support is refused to such schools or colleges as may be under specific religious control, while pension funds for the teachers, established by generous benefactions, are explicitly reserved for those who are on the faculties of institutions which formally dissociate themselves from any religious influence. I maintain that this is both unjust and against public policy. Under our present system of religious individualism and ecclesiastical multiplicity, approximations only are possible, but I believe the wise and just plan would be for the state to fix certain standards which all schools receiving financial support from the public funds must maintain, and then, this condition being carried out, distribute the funds received from general taxation to public and private schools alike. This would enable Episcopalians, let us say, or Roman Catholics, or Jews, when in any community they are numerous enough to provide a sufficiency of scholars for any primary, grammar, or high school, to establish such a school in as close a relationship to their own religion as they desired, and have this school maintained out of the funds of the city. This is not a purely theoretical proposition; after an agitation lasting nearly half a century, Holland has this year put such a law in force. From every point of view we should do well to recognize this plan as both just and expedient. One virtue it would have, apart from those already noted, is the variation it would permit in curricula, text books, personnel and scholastic life as between one school and another. There is no more fatal error in education than that standardization which has recently become a fad and which finds its most mechanistic manifestation in France.

Of course this need for the fortifying of education by religion is recognized even now, but the only plan devised for putting it into effect is one whereby various ministers of religion are allowed a certain brief period each week in which they may enter the public schools and give denominational instruction to those who desire their particular ministrations. This is one of the compromises, like the older method of Bible reading without commentary or exposition, which avails nothing and is apt to be worse than frank and avowed secularism. It is putting religion on exactly the same plane as analytical chemistry, psychoanalysis or salesmanship, (the latter I am told is about to be introduced in the Massachusetts high schools) or any other "elective," whereas if it is to have any value whatever it must be an ever-present force permeating the curriculum, the minds of the teachers, and the school life from end to end, and there is no way in which this can be accomplished except by a policy that will permit the maintenance of schools under religious domination at the expense of the state, provided they comply with certain purely educational requirements established and enforced by the state.

I have already pointed out what seems to me the desirability of a considerable variation between the curriculum of one school and another. This would be possible and probably certain under the scheme proposed, but barring this, it is surely an open question whether the pretty thoroughly standardized curriculum now in operation would not be considerably modified to advantage if it is recognized that the prime object of education is character rather than mental training and the fitting of a pupil to obtain a paying job on graduation. From my own point of view the answer is in a vociferous affirmative. I suggest the drastic reduction of the very superficial science courses in all schools up to and including the high school, certainly in chemistry, physics and biology, but perhaps with some added emphasis on astronomy, geology and botany. History should become one of the fundamental subjects, and English, both being taught for their humanistic value and not as exercises in memory or for the purpose of making a student a sort of dictionary of dates. This would require a considerable rewriting of history text books, as well as a corresponding change in the methods of teaching, but after all, are not these both consummations devoutly to be wished. There are few histories like Mr. Chesterton's "Short History of England," unfortunately. One would, perhaps, hardly commend this stimulating book as a sufficient statement of English history for general use in schools, but its approach is wholly right and it possesses the singular virtue of interest. Another thing that commends it is the fact that while it runs from Caesar to Mr. Lloyd George, it contains, I believe, only seven specific dates, three of which are possibly wrong. This is as it should be--not the inaccuracies but the commendable frugality in point of number. Dates, apart from a few key years, are of small historical importance; so are the details of palace intrigues and military campaigns. History is, or should be, life expressed in terms of romance, and it is of little moment whether the narrated incidents are established by documentary evidence or whether they are contemporary legend quite unsubstantiated by what are known (and overestimated) as "facts." There is more of the real Middle Ages in Mallory's "Mort d'Arthur" than there is in all Hallam, and the same antithesis can be established for nearly all other periods of history.

The history of man is one great dramatic romance, and so used it may be made perhaps the most stimulating agency in education as character development. I do not mean romance in the sense in which Mr. Wells takes it, that is to say, the dramatic assembling and clever coöordination of unsubstantiated theories, personal preferences, prejudices and aversions, under the guise of solemn and irrefutable truth attested by all the exact sciences known to man, but romance which aims like any other art at communicating from one person to another something of the inner and essential quality of life as it has been lived, even if the material used is textually doubtful or even probably apocryphal. The deadly enemy of good, sound history is scientific historical criticism. The true history is romantic tradition; the stimulating thing, the tale that makes the blood leap, the pictorial incident that raises up in an instant the luminous vision of some great thing that once was.

I would not exchange Kit Marlowe's

"Is this the face that launched a thousand ships
And burnt the topless towers of Ilium?"

for all the critical commentaries of Teutonic pedants on the character and attributes of Helen of Troy as these have (to them) been revealed by archaeological investigations. I dare say that Bishop St. Remi of Reims never said in so many words "Bow thy proud head, Sicambrian; destroy what thou hast worshipped, worship what thou hast destroyed," and that the Meroving monarch did not go thence to issue an "order of the day" that the army should forthwith march down to the river and be baptized by battalions; but *there* is the clear, unforgettable picture of the times and the men, and it will remain after the world has forgotten that some one has proved that St. Remi never met Clovis, and that he himself was probably only a variant of the great and original "sun-myth."

Closely allied with the teaching of history and forming a link as it were with the teaching of English, is a branch of study at present unformulated and unknown, but, I am convinced, of great importance in education as a method of character development. Life has always focused in great personalities, and formal history has recognized the fact while showing little discretion, and sometimes very defective judgment, in the choices it has made. A past period becomes our own in so far as we translate it through its personalities and its art; the original documents matter little, except when they become misleading, as they frequently do, when read through contemporary spectacles. Now the great figures of a time are not only princes and politicians, conquerors and conspirators, they are quite as apt to be the knights and heroes and brave gentlemen who held no conspicuous position in Church or state. I think we need what might be called "The Golden Book of Knighthood"--or a series of text books adapted to elementary and advanced schools--made up of the lives and deeds (whether attested by "original documents," or legendary or even fabulous does not matter) of those in all times, and amongst all peoples, who were the glory of knighthood; the "parfait gentyl Knyghtes" "without fear and without reproach." Such for example, to go no farther back than the Christian Era, as St. George and St. Martin, King Arthur and Launcelot and Galahad, Charles Martel and Roland, St. Louis, Godfrey de Bouillon and Saladin, the Earl of Strafford, Montrose and Claverhouse, the Chevalier Bayard, Don John of Austria, Washington and Robert Lee and George Wyndham. These are but a few names, remembered at random; there are scores besides, and I think that they should be held up to honour and emulation throughout the formative period of youth. After all, they became, during the years when these qualities were exalted, the personification of the ideals of honour and chivalry, of compassion and generosity, of service and self-sacrifice and courtesy, and these, the qualifications of a gentleman and a man or honour, are, with the religion that fostered them, and the practice of that religion, the just objective of education.

Much of all this can even now be taught through a judicious use of the opportunities offered instructors in English, whether this is through the graded "readers" of elementary education, or the more extended courses in colleges and universities. Very frequently these opportunities are ignored, and will be until we achieve something of a new orientation in the matter of teaching English.

Now it may be I hold a vain and untenable view of this subject, but I am willing to confess that I believe the object of teaching English is the unlocking of the treasures of thought, character and emotion preserved in the written records of the tongue, and the arousing of a desire to know and assimilate these treasures on the part of the pupil. I am very sure that English should not be taught as a thing ending in "ology," not as an intricate science with all sorts of laws and rules and exceptions; not as a system whereby the little children of the Ghetto, and the offspring of Pittsburgh millionaires, and the spectacled infant elect of Beacon Hill may all be raised to the point where they can write with acceptable fluency the chiseled phrases of Matthew Arnold, the cadenced Latinity of Sir Thomas Browne, the sonorous measures of Bolingbroke or the distinguished and resonant periods of the King James Bible. Such an aim as this will always result in failure.

The English language is the great storehouse of the rich thought and the burning emotion of the English race, and all this, as it has issued out of character, works towards the development of character, when it is made operative in new generations. There is no other language but Latin that has preserved so great a wealth of invaluable things, and English is taught in order that it all may be more available through that appreciation that comes from familiarity. There is no nobler record in the world: from Chaucer down to the moderns is one splendid sequence of character-revelations through a perfect but varied art, for literature is also a fine art, and one of the greatest of all. Is it not fair to say that the chief duty of the teacher of English is to lead the student to like great literature, to find it and enjoy it for himself, and through it to come to the liking of great ideas?

In the old days there was an historical, or rather archaeological, method that was popular; also an analytical and grammarian method. There was also the philological method which was quite the worst of all and had almost as devastating results as in the case of Latin. It almost seems as though English were being taught for the production of a community of highly specialized teachers. No one would now go back to any of those quaint and archaic ways digged up out of the dim and remote past of the XIXth century. We should all agree, I think, that for general education, specialized technical knowledge is unimportant and scientific intensive methods unjustifiable. For one student who will turn out a teacher there are five hundred that will be just simple voters, wage-earners, readers of the Saturday Evening Post and the New Republic, members of the Fourth Presbyterian Church or the Ethical Society, and respectable heads of families. The School of Pedagogy has its own methods (I am given to understand), but under correction I submit they are not those of general education. Shall I put the whole thing in a phrase and say that the object of teaching English is to get young people to like good things?

You may say this is English Literature, not English. Are the two so very far apart? English as a language is taught to make literature available. "Example is better than precept." Reading good literature for the love of it will bring in the habit of grammatical speaking and writing far more effectively than what is known as "a thorough grounding in the principles of English grammar." I doubt if the knowledge of, and facility in, English can be built up on such a basis; rather the laws should be deduced from examples. Philology, etymology, syntax are derivatives, not foundations. "Practice makes perfect" is a saying that needs to be followed by the old scholastic defensive *"distinguo."* Practice in reading, rather than practice in writing, makes good English composition possible. The "daily theme" may be overdone; it is of little use unless *thought* keeps ahead of the pen.

I would plead then for the teaching of English after a fashion that will reveal great thoughts and stimulate to greater life, through the noble art of English literature and the perfectly illogical but altogether admirable English language. The function of education is to make students feel, think and act, after a fashion that increasingly reveals and utilizes the best that is in them, and increasingly serves the uses of society, and both history and English can be so taught as to help towards the accomplishment of these ends.

There is another factor that may be so used, but I confess I shall speak of it with some hesitation. It is at present, and has been for ages, entirely outside the possibility even of consideration, and in a sense that goes beyond the general ignoring of religion, for while Catholics, who form the great majority of Christians, still hold to religion as a prime element in education, there are none--or only a minority so small as to be negligible--who give a thought to art in this connection. I bring forward the word, and the thing it represents, with diffidence, even apologetically: indeed, it is perhaps better to renounce the word altogether and substitute the term "beauty," for during the nineteenth century art got a bad name, not altogether undeservedly, and the disrepute lingers. So long as beauty is an instinct native to men (and it was this, except for very brief and periodic intervals, until hardly more than a century ago, though latterly in a vanishing form), it is wholesome, stimulating and indispensable, but when it becomes self-conscious, when it finds itself the possession of a few highly differentiated individuals instead of the attribute of man as such, then it tends to degenerate into something abnormal and, in its last estate, both futile and unclean. In its good estate, as for example in Greece, Byzantium, the Middle Ages, and in Oriental countries until the last few decades, beauty was so natural an object of endeavour and a mode of expression, and its universality resulted in so characteristic an environment, it was unnecessary to talk about it very much, or to give any particular thought to the educational value of the arts which were its manifestation through and to man, or how this was to be applied. The things were there, everywhere at hand; the temples and churches, the painting and the sculpture and the works of handicraft; the music and poetry and drama, the ceremonial and costume of daily life, both secular and religious, the very cities in which men congregated and the villages in which they were dispersed. Beauty, in all its concrete forms of art, was highly valued, almost as highly as religion or liberty or bodily health, but then it was a part of normal life and therefore taken for granted.

Now all is changed. For just an hundred years (the process definitely began here in America between 1820 and 1823) we have been eliminating beauty as an attribute of life and living until, during the last two generations, it is true to say that the instinctive impulse of the race as a whole is towards ugliness in those categories of creation and appreciation where formerly it had been towards beauty. Of course the corollary of this was the driving of the unhappy man in whom was born some belated impulse towards the apprehending of beauty and its visible expression in some art, back upon himself, until, conscious of his isolation and confident of his own superiority, he not only made his art a form of purely personal expression (or even of exposure), but held himself to be, and so conducted himself, as a being apart, for whom the laws of the herd were not, and to whom all men should bow.

The separation of art from life is only less disastrous in its results than the separation of religion from life, particularly since with the former went the separation of art (and therefore of beauty) from its immemorial alliance with religion. It was bad for art, it was bad for religion, and it was worst of all for life itself. Beyond a certain point man cannot live in and with and through ugliness, nor can society endure under such conditions, and the fact is that, however it came to pass, modern civilization has functioned through explicit ugliness, and the environment it has made for its votaries and its rebels indifferently, is unique in its palpable hideousness; from the clothes it wears and the motives it extols, to the cities it builds, and the structures therein, and the scheme of life that romps along in its ruthless career within the sordid suburbs that take the place of the once enclosing walls. And the defiant and segregated "artists," mortuary art museums, the exposed statues and hidden pictures, the opera subsidized by "high society," and the "arts and crafts" societies and the "art magazines" and "art schools" and clubs and "city beautiful" committees, only seem to make the contrast more apparent and the desperate nature of the situation more profound.

It is a new situation altogether, and nowhere in history is there any recorded precedent to which we can return for council and example, for nothing quite of the same sort ever happened before. It is also a problem of which formal education must take cognizance, for the lack is one which must somehow be supplied, while it reveals an astonishing *lacuna* in life that means a new deficiency in the unconscious education of man that renders him ineffective in life; defective even, it may be, unless from some source he can acquire something of what in the past life itself could afford.

Indeed it is not merely a negative influence we deal with, but a positive, for, to paraphrase a little, "ugly associations corrupt good morals." Youth is beaten upon at many points by things that not only look ugly, but are, and as in compassion we are bound to offer some new agency to fill a lack, so in self-defence we must take thought as to how the evil influence of contemporaneousness is to be nullified and its results corrected.

I confess the method seems to me to lean more closely to the indirect influence rather than the direct. It is doubtful if "art" can really be taught in any sense; the inherent sense of beauty can be fostered and an inherent aptitude developed, but that is about all. As for the building up of a non-professional passion for art I am quite sure it cannot be done, and should hardly be attempted, and very likely the same is true of the application of beauty.

Text books on "How to Understand" this art or that are interesting ventures into abstract theory, but they are little more. We must always remember that art is a result, not a product, and that sense of beauty is a natural gift and not an accomplishment. On the other hand, much can be accomplished by indirection, and by this I mean the buildings and the grounds and the cultural adjuncts that are offered by any school or college. The ordinary type of school-house--primary, grammar or high school--is, in its barren ugliness and its barbarous "efficiency," a very real outrage on decency, and a few Braun photographs and plaster casts and potted plants avail nothing. Private schools and some colleges--by no means all--are apt to be somewhat better, and here the improvement during the last ten years has been amazing, one or two universities having acquired single buildings, or groups, of the most astonishing architectural beauty. In no case, however, has as yet complete unity been achieved, while the arts of painting, sculpture, music and the drama, as vital and operative and pervasive influences, lag far behind, and formal religion with its liturgies and ceremonial, its constant and varied services and its fine and appealing pageantry--religion which is the greatest vitalizing and stimulating force in beauty is hardly touched at all.

Bad art of any kind is bad anywhere, but in any type of educational institution, from the kindergarten to the post graduate college, it is worse and less excusable than it is elsewhere, unless it be in association with religion, while the absence of beauty at the instigation of parsimony or efficiency is just as bad. I am firmly persuaded that we need, not more courses of study but more beautiful environment for scholars under instruction.

I have touched cursorily on certain elements in education which need either a new emphasis or an altogether new interpretation; religion, history, art, but this does not mean that the same treatment should not be accorded elsewhere. There are certain studies that should be revived, such as formal logic, there are others that need immediate and complete restoration, as Latin for example, there are many, chiefly along scientific and vocational lines, that could well be minimized, or in some cases dispensed with altogether: one might go on indefinitely on this line, however, weighing and testing studies in relation to their character-value, but certainly enough has already been said to indicate the point of view I would urge for consideration. Before I close, however, I want to touch on two points that arise in connection with college education, if, even for the sake of argument, we admit that the primary object of all formal education is the "education" of the character-capacity in each individual.

Of these two, the first has to do with the college curriculum, but I need to devote little time to this for the principle has already been developed and applied in a singularly stimulating and lucid book called "The Liberal College," by President Meiklejohn of Amherst, to which I beg to refer you. The scheme is a remarkable blending of the prescribed and the elective systems, and provides for the freshman year five compulsory studies, viz.: Social and Economic Institutions, Mathematics and Formal Logic, Science, English and Foreign Languages; for the sophomore year European History, Philosophy, Science, Literature, and one elective; for the junior year American History, History of Thought and two electives, and for the senior year one required study, Intellectual and Moral Problems, and one elective, the latter, which takes two-thirds of the student's time, must be a continuation of one of the four subjects included in the junior year. It seems to me that this is a singularly wise programme, since it not only determines the few studies which are fundamental, and imposes them on the student in diminishing number as he advances in his work, but it also provides for that freedom of choice which permits any student to find out and continue the particular line along which his inclinations lead him to travel, until his senior year is chiefly given over to the fullest possible development of the special subject. The fad for free electives all along the line was one of those curious phenomena, both humorous and tragic, that grew out of the evolutionary philosophy and the empirical democracy of the nineteenth century, and it wrought disaster, while the ironclad curriculum that preceded it was almost as bad along an opposite line. This project of Dr. Meiklejohn's seems to me to recognize life as a force and to base itself on this sure foundation instead of on the shifting sands of doctrinaire theory, and if this is so then it is right.

For after all there is such a thing as life, and it is more potent than theory as it also has a way of disregarding or even smashing the machine. It is this force of life that should be more regarded in education, and more relied upon. It is the living in a school or a college that counts more than a curriculum; the association with others, students and teachers, the communal life, the common adventures and scrapes, the common sports, yes, and as it will be sometime, the common worship. It is through these that life works and character develops, and to this development and instigation of life the school and college should work more assiduously, minimizing for the moment the problems of curricula and pedagogic methods. If I am right in this there is no place for the "correspondence school," while the college or university that numbers its students by thousands becomes at least of doubtful value, and perhaps impossible. In any case it seems to me self-evident that a college, whatever its numbers, must have, as its primal and essential units, self-contained groups of not more than 150 students segregated in their own residential quad, with its common-room, refectory and chapel, and with a certain number of faculty members in residence, the whole being united under one "head." There may be perhaps no reason why, granting this unit system, these should not be multiplied in number until the whole student body is as great as that of a western state university today, but to me the idea is abhorrent of an "university" with five or ten thousand students all jostling together In one inchoate mass, eating in numerical mobs, assembling in social "unions" as large as a metropolitan hotel and almost as homelike, or taking refuge for safety from mere numbers in clubs, fraternities and secret societies. A college such as this is a mob, not an organism, and as a mob it ought to be put down.

I said at the outset of this lecture that we could not lay the present failure of civilization to the doors of education, however great its shortcomings, for the causes lay deeper than this. I maintain that this is true; and yet formal education can not escape scatheless, for it has failed to admit this decline while acknowledging the claim set up for it that it could and would achieve this end. Certainly it will incur a heavy responsibility if it does not at once recognize the fact that while it can not do the half that has been claimed for it, it can do far more than it is doing now, and that in a very large degree the future does depend for its honour or its degradation on the part formal education is to perform at the present crisis. To do this it must execute a ***volte face*** and confess that it can only develop inherent potential, not create capacity, and that the primary object of its activities must be not the stall-feeding of intellect and the practical preparation for a business career, but the fostering and the building up of the personal character that denotes the Christian gentleman. I do not think that I can do better for a conclusion than to quote from the "Philosophy of Education" by the late Dr. Thomas Edward Shields.

"The unchanging aim of Christian education is, and always has been, to put the pupil into possession of a body of truth derived from nature and from Divine Revelation, from the concrete work of man's hand and from the content of human speech, in order to bring his conduct into conformity with Christian ideals and with the standards of the civilization of his day.

"Christian education, therefore, aims at transforming native instincts while preserving and enlarging their powers. It aims at bringing the flesh under the control of the spirit. It draws upon the experience and the wisdom of the race, upon Divine Revelation and upon the power of Divine grace, in order that it may bring the conduct of the individual into conformity with Christian ideals and with the standards of the civilization of the day. It aims at the development of the whole man, at the preservation of unity and continuity in his conscious life; it aims at transforming man's native egotism to altruism; at developing the social side of his nature to such an extent that he may regard all men as his brothers; sharing with them the common Fatherhood of God. In one word, it aims at transforming a child of the flesh into a child of God."

VII
THE PROBLEM OF ORGANIC RELIGION

If philosophy is "the science of the totality of things," and "they are called wise who put things in their right order and control them well," then it is religion, above all other factors and potencies, that enters in to reveal the right relationships and standards of value, and to contribute the redemptive and energizing force that makes possible the adequate control which is the second factor in the conduct of the man that is "called wise." Philosophy and religion are not to be confounded; religion is sufficient in itself and develops its own philosophy, but the latter is not sufficient in itself, and when it assumes the functions and prerogatives of religion, it brings disaster.

Religion is the force that relates action to life. Of course it has other aspects, higher in essence and more impalpable in quality, but it is this first aspect I shall deal with, because I am not now speaking of religion as a purely spiritual power but only of its quality as the great coordinator of human action, the power that establishes a right ratio of values and gives the capacity for right control. Whether we accept the religion of the Middle Ages or not; whether we look on the period as one of high and edifying Christian civilization, or as a time of ignorance and superstition, we are bound to admit that society in its physical, intellectual and spiritual aspects was highly organized, and coordinated after a most masterly fashion. It was more nearly an unit, functioning lucidly and consistently, than anything the world has known since the Roman Empire. Whatever its defects, lack of coherency was not one of them. Life was not divided into water-tight compartments, but moved on as a consistent whole. Failures were constant, for the world even then was made up of men, but the ideal was perfectly clear-cut, the principles exactly seen and explicitly formulated; life was organic, consistent, highly articulated, and withal as full of the passion of aspiration towards an ultimate ideal as was the Gothic cathedral which is its perfect exemplar.

The reason for this coherency and consistency was the universal recognition and acceptance of religion as the one energizing and standardizing force in life, the particular kind of religion that then prevailed, and the organic power which this religion had established; that is to say, the Church as an operative institution. So long as this condition obtained, which was, roughly speaking, for three hundred years, from the "Truce of God" in 1041 to the beginning of the "Babylonian Captivity" of the Papacy at Avignon in 1309, there was substantial unity in life, but as soon as it was shaken, this unity began to break up into a diversity that accomplished a condition of chaos, at and around the opening of the sixteenth century, which only yielded to the absolutism of the Renaissance, destined in its turn to break up into a second condition of chaos under the influence of industrialism, Puritanism and revolution.

Since the accomplishment of the Reformation, this function of religion has never been restored to society in any degree comparable with that which it maintained during the Middle Ages. The Counter-Reformation preserved the institution itself in the Mediterranean lands, but it did not restore its old spiritual power in its entirety. Amongst the peoples that accepted the Reformation the new religion assumed for a time the authority of the old, but the centrifugal force inherent in its nature soon split the reformed churches into myriad fragments, so destroying their power of action, while the abandonment of the sacramental system progressively weakened their dynamic force. As it had from the first compounded, under compulsion, with absolutism and tyranny, so in the end it compromised with the cruelty, selfishness, injustice and avarice of industrialism, and when finally this achieved world supremacy, and physical science, materialistic philosophy and social revolution entered the field as co-combatants, it no longer possessed a sufficient original power either of resistance or of re-creative energy.

Religion is in itself not the reaction of the human mind, under process of evolution, to certain physical stimuli of experience and phenomena, it is supernatural in that its source is outside nature; it is a manifestation of the grace of God, and as such it cannot be brought into existence by any conscious action of man or by any of his works. On the other hand, it can be fostered and preserved, or debilitated and dispersed, by these human acts and institutions, and in the same way man himself may be made more receptive to this divine grace, or turned against it, by the same agencies, the teachings of Dr. John Calvin to the contrary notwithstanding. This is part of the Catholic doctrine of free-will as opposed to the sixteenth-century dogma of predestination which, distorted and degraded from the doctrine of St. Paul and St. Augustine, played so large a part in that transformation of the Christian religion from which we have suffered ever since. God offers the free gift of religion and of faith to every child of man, but the recipient must cooperate if the gift is to be accepted. The Church, that is to say, the supernatural organism that is given material form in time and space and operates through human agencies, is for this reason subject to great vicissitudes, now rising to the highest level of righteousness and power, now sinking into depths of unrighteousness and impotence. Nothing, however, can affect the validity and the potency of its supernatural content and its supernatural channels of grace. These remain unaffected, whether the human organism is exalted or debased. The sacraments and devotions and practices of worship, are in themselves as potent if a Borgia sits in the chair of St. Peter as they are if a Hildebrand, and Innocent III or a Leo XIII is the occupant; nevertheless every weakening or degradation of the visible organism affects, and inevitably, the attitude of men towards the thing itself, and when this declension sets in and continues unchecked, the result is, first, a falling away and a discrediting of religion that sometimes results in general abandonment, and second--and after a time--a new outpouring of spiritual power that results in complete regeneration. The Church, in its human manifestation, is as subject to the rhythmical rise and fall of the currents of life as is the social organism or man himself, therefore it is not to be expected that it will pursue a course of even exaltation, or maintain a status that is impeccable.

Now the working out of this law had issue in a great decline that began with the Exile at Avignon and was not terminated until the Council of Trent. In the depth of this catastrophe came the natural and righteous revolt against the manifold and intolerable abuses, but, like all reforming movements that take on a revolutionary character, reform and regeneration were soon forgotten in the unleashed passion for destruction and innovation, while the new doctrines of emancipation from authority, and the right of private judgment in religious matters, were seized upon by sovereigns chafing under ecclesiastical control, as a providential means of effecting and establishing their own independence, and so given an importance, and an ultimate victory that, in and by themselves, they could hardly have achieved. In the end it was the secular and autocratic state that reaped the victory, not the reformed religion, which was first used as a tool and then abandoned to its inevitable break-up into numberless antagonistic sects, some of them retaining a measure of the old faith and polity, others representing all the illiteracy and uncouthness and fanaticism of the new racial and social factors as these emerged at long last from the submergence and the oppression that had been their fate with the dissolution of Mediaevalism.

Meanwhile the Roman Church which stood rigidly for historic Christianity and had been preserved by the Counter-Reformation to the Mediterranean states, continued bound to the autocratic and highly centralized administrative system that had become universal among secular powers during the decadence of Mediaevalism, and from which it had taken its colour, and it kept even pace for the future with the progressive intensification of this absolutism. This was natural, though in many respects deplorable, and it can be safely said that adverse criticism of the Catholic Church today is based only on qualities it acquired during the period of Renaissance autocracy and revived paganism; qualities that do not affect its essential integrity or authority but do misrepresent it before men, and work as a handicap in its adaptability and in its work of winning souls to Christianity and re-establishing the unity of Christendom. Fortunately this very immobility has saved it from a surrender to the new forces that were developed in secular society during the last two centuries, as it did yield to the compulsion of those that were let loose in the two that preceded them. It has never subjected questions of faith and morals to popular vote nor has it determined discipline by parliamentary practice under a well developed party system, therefore it has preserved its unity, its integrity and its just standard of comparative values. On the other hand, it has held so stubbornly to some of the ill ways of Renaissance centralization, which are in no sense consonant with its character, that it has failed to retard the constant movement of society away from a life wherein religion was the dominating and coordinating force, while at the present crisis it is as yet hardly more able than a divisive Protestantism to offer the regenerative energy that a desperate case demands.

I do not know whether secular society is responsible for the decadence of religion, or the decadence of religion is responsible for the failure of secular society, nor does it particularly matter. What I am concerned with is a condition amounting to almost complete severance between the two, and how we may "knit up this ravelled sleeve" of life so that once more we may have an wholesome unity in place of the present disunity; for until this is accomplished, until once more religion enters into the very marrow of social being, enters with all its powers of judgment and determination and co-ordination and creative energy, just so long shall we seek in vain for our way out into the Great Peace of righteous and consistent living.

Of course there is only one sure way, one method by which this, and all our manifold difficulties, can be resolved, and that is through the achieved enlightenment of the individual. As I have insisted in each of these lectures, salvation is not through machinery but through the individual soul, for it is life itself that is operating, not the instruments that man devises in his ingenuity. Yet the mechanism is of great value for even itself may give aid and stimulus in the personal regenerative process, or, on the contrary, it may deter this by the confusing and misleading influences it creates. Therefore we are bound to regard material reforms, and of these, as they suggest themselves in the field of organized religion, I propose to speak.

No one will deny the progressive alienation of life from religion that has developed since the Reformation and has now reached a point of almost complete severance. Religion, once a public preoccupation, has now withdrawn to the fastnesses of the individual soul, when it has not vanished altogether, as it has in the case of the majority of citizens of this Republic in so far as definite faith, explicit belief, application, practice and action are concerned. In the hermitage that some still make within themselves, religion still lives on as ardent and as potent and as regenerative as before, but in general, if we are to judge from the conduct of recent life, it is held, when it is accepted at all, with a certain formality, and is neither cherished with conviction nor allowed to interfere with the everyday life of the practical man. As a great English statesman remarked in the last century, "No one has a higher regard for religion than I, but when it comes to intruding it into public affairs, well, really--!"

The situation is one not unnaturally to be anticipated, for the whole course of religious, secular and sociological development during the last few centuries has been such as to make any other result improbable. I already have tried to show what seem to me the destructive factors, secularly and sociologically. As for the factors in religious development that have worked towards the same end, they are, first, the shattering of the unity of Christendom, with the denial by those of the reformed religions of the existence of a Church, one, visible and Catholic and infallible in matters of faith and morals; second, the denial of sacramental philosophy and abandonment of the sacraments (or all but one, or at most two of them) as instruments of Divine Grace; third, the surrender of the various religious organisms to the compulsion of the materialistic, worldly and opportunist factors in the secular life of modernism. The truths corresponding to these three errors are, Unity, Sacramentalism and Unworldliness. Until these three things are won back, Christianity will fail of its full mission, society will continue aimless, uncooerdinate and on the verge of disaster, life itself will lack the meaning and the reality that give both joy in the living and victory in achievement, while the individual man will be gravely handicapped in the process of personal regeneration.

It is not my purpose to frame a general indictment against persons and movements, but rather to suggest certain ways and means of possible recovery, and in general I shall try to confine myself to that form of organized religion to which I personally adhere, that is to say, the Anglican or Episcopal Church, partly because of my better knowledge of its conditions, and partly because whatever is said may in most cases be equally well applied to the Protestant denominations.

The unity of the Church. It is no longer necessary to demonstrate this fundamental necessity. The old days of the nineteenth century are gone, those days when honest men vociferously acclaimed as honourable and glorious "the dissidence of dissent and the protestantism of the Protestant religion." Everyone knows now, everyone, that is, that accepts Christianity, that disunion is disgrace if not a very palpable sin. The desire for a restored unity is almost universal, but every effort in this direction, whatever its source, meets with failure, and the reason would appear to be that the approach is made from the wrong direction. In every case the individual is left alone, his personal beliefs and practices are, he is assured, jealously guarded; all that is asked is that some mechanical amalgamation, some official approximation shall be effected.

Free interchange of pulpits, a system of reciprocal re-ordination, a "merger" of church property and parsons, an "irreducible minimum" of credal insistencies these, and others even more ingeniously compromising, are the well-meaning schemes that are put forward, and in the process one point after another is surrendered, as a *quid pro quo* for the formal and technical capitulation of some other religious group.

It is demonstrable that even if these well-meaning approximations were received with favour--and thus far nothing of the kind has appeared--the result, so far as essential unity is concerned, would be *nil.* There is a perfectly definite line of division between the Catholic and the Protestant, and until this line is erased there is no possible unity, even if this were only official and administrative. The Catholic (and in respect to this one particular point I include under this title members of the Roman, Anglican and Eastern Communions) maintains and practices the sacramental system; the Protestant does not. There is no reason, there is indeed grave danger of sacrilege, in a joint reception of the Holy Communion by those who look on it as a mere symbol and those who accept it as the very Body and Blood of Christ. Protestant clergy are urged to accept ordination at the hands of Anglican bishops, but the plea is made on the ground of order, expediency, and the preservation of tradition; whereas the Apostolical succession was established and enforced not for these reasons but in order that the grace of God, originally imparted by Christ Himself, may be continued through the lines He ordained, for the making and commissioning of priests who have power to serve as the channels for the accomplishing of the divine miracle of the Holy Eucharist, to offer the eternal Sacrifice of the Body and Blood of Christ for the quick and the dead, and to remit the penalty of sins through confession and absolution. If the laying on of hands by the bishop were solely a matter of tradition and discipline, neither Rome nor the Anglican Communion would be justified in holding to it as a condition of unity; if it is for the transmission of the Holy Ghost for the making of a Catholic priest, with all that implies and has always implied, then it is wrong, even in the interests of a formal unity, to offer it to those who believe neither in the priesthood nor in the sacraments in the Catholic and historic sense.

The conversion of the individual must take precedence of corporate action of any sort. When the secularist comes to believe in the Godhead of Christ he will unite himself with the rest of the faithful in a Church polity, but he will not do this, he has too much self-respect, simply because he is told by some ardent but minimizing parson that he does not have to believe in the Divinity of Christ in order to "join the church." When a Protestant comes to accept the sacramental system, to desire to participate in the Holy Sacrifice of the altar, to make confession of his sins and receive absolution, and to nourish and develop his spiritual nature by the use of the devotions that have grown up during nineteen hundred years, he will renounce his Protestantism, when his self-respect would not permit him to do this just because he had been assured that he need not really change any of his previous beliefs in order to ally himself with a Church that had better architecture and a more artistic ceremonial, and locally a higher social standing. When Anglicans or the Eastern Orthodox come to believe that a vernacular liturgy and a married priesthood and provincial autonomy are of less importance than Catholic unity, and when Roman Catholics can see that the same is of greater moment than a rigid preservation of Renaissance centralization and a cold *"non possumus"* in the matter of Orders, then the way will be open for the reunion of the West, where this operation cannot be affected by formal negotiations looking towards some form of legalistic concordat.

The evil heritage of the sixteenth century is still heavy upon us, and this heritage is one of jealousy and hate, not of charity and toleration. It is an heritage of legalism and technicalities, of self-will and individualism, of shibboleths that have become a dead letter, of prejudices that are fostered on distorted history and the propaganda of the self-seeking and the vain. The spirit of Christ is not in it, but the malice of Satan working upon the better natures of men and justifying in the name of conscience and principle what are frequently the workings of self-will and pride and intellectual obsession. This is the tragedy of it all; that Protestants and Anglicans and Roman Catholics are, so far as the majority are concerned, honestly convinced that they are right in maintaining their own divisiveness; in perpetuating an hundred Protestant sects on the basis of some variation in the form of baptism or church government or the method of conversion; in splitting up the Catholic Church because of a thousand year old disagreement as to a clause in the Creed which has a technical and theological significance only, or because one sector is alleged to have added unjustifiably to the Faith while the other is alleged to have unjustifiably taken away. Self-will and lack of charity, not love and the common will as these are revealed to the world through the Divine Will of Christ, are working here. The momentary triumph of evil over good, the passing victory that yet means the banishment of religion from the world, and the assurance of disaster still greater than that which is now upon us unless every man bends all his energies to the task of making the will of God prevail, first in himself, and so in the secular and ecclesiastical societies in and through which he plays his part in the life of the world--these are the fruits of a divided Christendom.

I honestly believe that the first real step towards reunion would be a prompt cessation of the whole process of criticism, vilification and abuse, one of the other, that now marks the attitude of what are known as "church periodicals." Roman, Anglican, Protestant, are all alike, for all maintain a consistent slanging of each other. I have in mind in particular weekly religious papers in the United States which maintain departments almost wholly made up of attacks on Roman Catholicism and the derision of incidents of bad taste or illiteracy in the Protestant denominations, and others which lose no opportunity to discredit or abuse the Episcopal Church and the Protestant denominations, and finally a curiously malevolent newspaper representing the worst type of Protestant ignorance and prejudice, which exists on its libelous and indecent and dishonest assaults on Catholicism wherever it may be found. These are not alone, for the condition of ascerbity and nagging is practically universal. It merely echoes the pulpit and a portion of the general public. We all know of the so called "church" in Boston that is the forum of "escaped nuns" and "unfrocked priests," but in many places of better repute the sermon that bitterly attacks Christian Science, or "High Church Episcopalianism," or the errors of Protestantism generally, or the "usurpations of Rome" is by no means unknown, while elsewhere than in Ireland, the public as a whole finds much pleasure in bating any religion that happens to differ from its own,--or offends its sense of the uselessness of all religion. Let us have a new "Truce of God," and for the space of a year let all clergy, lecturers, newspapers, religious journals, and private individuals, totally abstain from sneering and ill-natured attacks on other religions and their followers. Could this be accomplished a greater step would be taken towards the reunion of Christendom than could be achieved by any number of conferences, commissions, councils and conventions.

It was the will and the intent of Christ "that they all may be one, that the world may believe that Thou hast sent Me," and in disunity we deny Christ. There is no consideration of inheritance, of personal taste, of interests, of intellectual persuasion that can stand in the way of an affirmative answer to this prayer. Every man who calls himself a Christian and yet is not praying and working to break down the self-will and the self-conceit that, so often under the masquerade of conscience, hold him back from a return, even if it is only step by step, to the original unity of the Catholic Faith, is guilty of sin, while it is sin of an even graver degree that stands to the account of those who consciously work to perpetuate the division that now exists.

Sacramentalism. The stumbling block, the apparently impassable barrier, is that which was erected when belief was substituted for faith; it is the intellectualizing of religion that has brought about the present failure of Christianity as a vital and controlling force in man and in society. The danger revealed itself even in the Middle Ages, and through perhaps the greatest Christian philosopher, and certainly one of the most commanding intellects, the world has known: St. Thomas Aquinas. In his case, and that of the others of his time, the intellect was still directed by spiritual forces, the chiefest of which was faith, therefore the inherent danger in the intellectualizing process did not clearly reveal itself or come into actual operation, but with the Renaissance and the Reformation it stood boldly forth, and since then as mind increased in its dominion faith declined. The Reformation, in all its later phases, that is to say, after it ceased to be a protest against moral defects and administrative abuses and became a revolutionary invention of new dogmas and practices, was the result of clever, stupid or perverse minds working overtime on religious problems which could not be solved or even apprehended by the intellect, whether it was that of an acute and highly trained master such as Calvin, or that of any one of the hundred founders of less savage but more curious and uncouth types of "reformed religion."

What we need now for the recovery and re-establishment of Christianity is not so much increased belief as it is a renewed faith; faith in Christ, faith in His doctrine, faith in His Church. We lost this faith when we abandoned the sacraments and sacramentalism as superstitions, or retained some of them in form and as symbols while denying to them all supernatural power. If we would aid the individual soul to regain this lost faith we could do no better than to restore the seven sacraments of the historic Christian faith, and Christian Church to the place they once held for all Christians, and still hold in the Roman Catholic Church, the Eastern Orthodox

Churches and (with limitations) in the Anglican Church. Faith begets faith; faith in Christ brings faith in the sacraments, and faith in the sacraments brings faith in Christ.

It is disbelief in the efficacy of the sacraments and in the sacramental principle in life that is the essential barrier between Protestantism and Catholicism, and until this barrier is dissolved there can be neither formal unity nor unity by compromise. This is already widely recognized, and as well the actual loss that comes with the denial and abandonment of the sacraments. There is in the Presbyterian church of Scotland a strong tendency towards a reassertion of the full sacramental doctrine; the "Free Catholic" movement throughout Great Britain is made up of Congregationalists, Methodists, Baptists, and other representatives of Evangelical Protestantism, and it is working unreservedly for the recovery and application of all the Catholic sacraments, with the devotions and ritual that go with them. Dr. Orchard, the head, and a Congregational minister, maintains in London a church where, as a Methodist member of the "Free Catholic" organization wrote me the other day, "the Blessed Sacrament is perpetually reserved and 'High Mass' is celebrated on Sundays with the full Catholic ceremonial." In my own practice of architecture I am constantly providing Presbyterian, Congregational, and even Unitarian churches, by request, with chancels containing altars properly vested and ornamented with crosses and candles, while the almost universal demand is for church edifices that shall approach as nearly as possible in appearance to the typical Catholic church of the Middle Ages. Of course some of this is due to a revived instinct for beauty, that almost sacramental quality in life which was ruthlessly destroyed by Protestantism, and also to a renewed sense of the value of symbol and ritual; but back of it all is the growing consciousness that, as Dr. Newman Smythe says, Protestantism has definitely failed, or at least become superannuated; that the essence of religion is spiritual not intellectual, affirmative not negative, and that the only measure of safety lies in a return towards, if not actually to, the Catholic faith and practice from which the old revolt was affected. It is a movement both significant and full of profound encouragement.

Here then are two tendencies that surely show the way and demand encouragement and furtherance; recovery of the sense of Christian unity in Christ and through an united Catholic Church, and the re-acceptance of sacramentalism as the expression of that faith and as the method of that Church. I feel very strongly that wherever these tendencies show themselves they must be acclaimed and cherished. The Protestant denominations must be aided in every way in their process of recovery of the good things once thrown away; Episcopalians must be persuaded that nothing can be wrong that leads souls to Christ, and that therefore they must cease their opposition to Reservation of the Blessed Sacrament explicitly for adoration, to such devotions as Benediction and the Rosary simply because they have not explicit Apostolic sanction, or to vestments, incense and holy water because certain prescriptive laws passed four hundred years ago in England have never been repealed. Above all is it necessary that the Episcopal Church should declare itself formally for the reinstitution of the seven Catholic sacraments, with the Mass as the one supreme act of worship, obligatory as the chief service on Sundays and Holy Days, and both as communion and as sacrifice. In this connection there is one reform that would I think be more effective than any other, (except the exaltation of the Holy Eucharist itself) and that is the complete cessation of the practice of commissioning lay readers and using them for mission work and clerical assistance. A mission can be established and made fruitful only on the basis of the sacraments, and chiefly on those of the Holy Eucharist and Penance. It is not enough to send a zealous and well intentioned layman to "a promising mission field" in order that he may read Morning and Evening Prayer and some sermon already published. What is needed is a priest to say Mass and hear confessions, and nothing else will serve as a substitute. How this is to be accomplished, now when the candidates for Holy Orders are constantly falling off in number, with no immediate prospect of recovery, is a question. Perhaps we may learn something from the old custom of ordaining "Mass priests," without cure of souls and with a commission to celebrate the Holy Mysteries even while they continue their own secular work in the world. For my own part I am persuaded that the best solution lies in the establishing of diocesan monasteries where men may take vows for short terms, and, during the period of these vows, remain at the orders of the bishop to go out at any time and anywhere in the diocese and to do such temporary or periodical mission work as he may direct.

Unworldliness: I have referred to the great falling off in the number of candidates for the priesthood in the Episcopal Church; the same phenomenon is apparent in all the Protestant denominations, so far as I know, but it has not shown itself in the Roman Catholic Church. This defection parallels the falling-off of membership in the various churches (except again the Roman Catholic) in proportion to the increase in population. We are told that the diminution of the ministry is due to the starvation wages that are paid in the vast majority of cases, and of course it is true that where a married clergy is allowed, men who believe they have a calling both to ministerial and to domestic life will think twice before they follow the call of the first when the pecuniary returns are such as to make the second impossible, which is, generally speaking, the situation today. To obviate this difficulty many religious bodies have recently established pension funds, but even this form of clerical insurance, together with the increase that has been effected in clerical stipends, has shown no results in an increase of students in theological seminaries and in candidates for Orders. The man who has enough of faith in God and a strong enough call to the ministry of Christ, will answer the call even if he does think twice before doing so. The trouble lies, I believe, in the very lack of faith and in a failure of confidence in organized religion largely brought about by organized religion itself through the methods it has pursued during the last two or three generations. There is a widespread belief that it is compromising with the world; that it is playing fast and loose with faith and discipline in a vain opportunism that voids it of spiritual power. Even where distrust does not reach this disastrous conclusion, there is a growing feeling of repugnance to the methods now being adopted in high quarters to "sell religion" to the public, as is the phrase which is sufficient in itself to explain the falling away that now seems to be in process. The attempt to win unwilling support by the methods of the "institutional church," the rampant advertising, so frequently under the management of paid "publicity agents"; the setting apart of half the Sundays in the year for some one or other special purpose, usually the raising of money for a specific and frequently worthy object; the "drives" for millions, the huge and impressive organizations, "scientifically" conducted, for rounding up lapsed communicants, or doubtful converts, or cash and pledges for missions, or pensions, or the raising of clergy stipends; the "Nation-wide Campaign," the "Inter-Church World Movement"; these--not to speak of the growing policy of "making it easy" for the hesitant to "come into the church" by minimizing unpopular clauses in the Creeds or loosening-up on discipline, and of attracting "advanced" elements by the advocacy and exploiting of each new social or industrial or political fad as it arises--are strong deterrents to those who honestly and ardently hunger for religion that *is* religion and neither social service nor "big business."

Christ said "you **cannot** serve both God and mammon," and this is one of the few cases where He stated a moral condition as a fact instead of indicating the right or the wrong possibility in action. Organized Christianity has for some time been trying to render this dual service, and the penalty thereof is now on the world. This consideration seems to me so important and so near the root of our troubles, and not in the field of organized religion alone, that I am going to quote at length from the Rev. Fr. Duffy of the American "Society of the Divine Compassion." What he has said came to me while I was preparing this lecture, and it is so much better than anything I could say that for my present purpose I make it my own.

"To the thoughtful person, and the need of reformation will appeal only to the thoughtful person, it must on reflection become abundantly evident that the chief necessity of our times in the religious world is the recovery of Faith. Probably lack of the true measure of Faith has been the story of every generation, with few exceptions, in the long history of Christianity, but there possibly never has been a time when men talked more of it and possessed less than in our own day. * * * *"

"Christianity is a new thing of splendid vision for each and every generation of men, unique in its promise and unapproached in its attraction. And yet how small a factor we have made it in the world's moulding compared with what it might be. We have not achieved a tiny part of what we might have achieved, because we lack the essentials of achievement; Faith and Faith's vision. Obsessed, after centuries of discussion and persecution, with the notion that faith is made up of mere belief, we have lost the secret of that victorious power that overcomes the world, and are weakly dependent upon the world's means for what spiritual operation we undertake. And so content have we grown with things as they are, that what they might be comes only as a dream that passes away quickly with the night; blind to our appalling money-dependency in modern religion, satisfied that the Kingdom of Heaven is as nigh to us as is possible under present conditions of society, we practically have substituted for the theological virtues, Faith, Hope and Charity, the ascending degrees of belief, resignation, money. This is partly due to our religious inheritance and partly to mental and spiritual sloth which dislikes the effort of thinking, preferring easy acquiescence in conditions that are the resultants of blinded vision. For dependency upon money is not something merely of the present, but a condition in the spiritual sphere that is largely a product of a long past. The really inexcusable thing is our willingness, in a day of greater light and knowledge, to close our eyes to the true nature of the unattractive, anaemic thing we *call* faith, which would be seen as powerless to achieve at all, if taken out of the soil of material means in which it has been planted."

He then gives various instances of methods actually put in practice amongst the churches and denominations which indicate the renunciation of faith and an exclusive reliance on worldy agencies and he then continues:

"The Joint Commission on Clergy Pensions, appointed by the General Convention of 1913, made as the basis for apportionment, not the services of self-denial of, but the amount of stipend received by, the clergy eligible for pension, thus penalizing the priest who, for the love of God, sacrificed a larger income to accept work in the most needed places where toil is abundant and money scarce. It must be evident, of course, that the motive of the Commission is not an endorsement of the blasphemous gospel of Success, by adding penalty to the self-denying clergy; what is painfully obvious is their apparent unbounded confidence that there are no clergy sufficiently foolish to sacrifice stipend at the call of faith's venture! And since the Armistice, the only real activity in organized religion has been a series of "drives" for vast sums of money, in most cases professionally directed.

"A consideration of a few facts such as the forgoing must readily convince even the most unimaginative person that whatever power faith might have had in the past, it counts for little today; that its secrets, its very meaning have been forgotten. Otherwise there could not be this extraordinary exaggeration of the place of money in spiritual operation, and the unblushing, tacit admission that mammon, which Christ so warned against, had been recognized as the master of spiritual situation, instead of the willing servant and useful adjunct of faith it was designed to be in the Christian vision. Indeed they all speak of that, largely unconscious, atmosphere of distrust of God which is so all-prevailing among Christian people today. If the great, positive vice of the age is covetousness, the great negative one is distrust of God; the two invariably go together as parts of a whole--one is the reverse side of the other--for, it is not that we *must* not, or *ought* not, but that we "cannot serve God and mammon." And this atmosphere is one in which faith cannot exist, it is stifled, crushed, killed, except it breathe the pure, sweet air of God, with which it can alone surround itself when human hearts will.

"It is not surprising that out of such conditions should grow false values, and that spirituality should be measured by the world's standard. Thus we have fallen into the vicious habit of adjudging qualifications for spiritual leadership among the clergy by the amount of their stipends, and measuring their potentialities for usefulness in the Kingdom of God by the amount of their yearly incomes; among the laity, the men of power are ever the men of material means, whom we permit to play the part of Providence in feeding and sustaining the Church from large purses, the filling of which will not always bear close investigation, and the really successful parish is always the one that, no matter what its spiritual condition, rejoices in abundant material means. So evident is it that the means of spiritual life have been so confused with the purely material, that it occasions no surprise when a neighbourhood having changed from the residence district of the comparatively well-to-do to the very poor, the vestry feels bound to consider the moving of the church to a more 'desirable' quarter.

"These, of course, are hard facts to face, and it is not strange that we should seek to evade them by a false optimism that thinks evil is eliminated by merely contemplating good. The point is, ***they must be faced,*** and at a time when there is some evidence of a little awakening, it must more and more force itself into the consciousness of the thoughtful that the dead spiritual conditions of today are due to the shifting of faith from God to material things as the means of achieving. The only hope lies in the apparent unconsciousness of the error. This is invariably the atmosphere that prevails when ecclesiastical history repeats itself in corruption; it had been true of more than two or three generations, though obviously unseen save by a few of those contemporary with the times, that in Jerusalem, 'the heads thereof judge for reward, and the priests teach for hire, and the prophets thereof divine for money; yet will they lean upon the Lord, and say: Is not the Lord among us? None evil can come upon us.' Corporate unconsciousness, in greater or less measure, of these conditions, may influence the degree of guilt, but never can acquit of the sin. And the cold, naked truth is that today we stand almost helpless before a world of peculiar problems.

"What is there here to reflect the ***power*** and ***might*** of Christianity, such as the early Church, especially, possessed, and subsequent generations, in times of great faith, really knew so much of--the power to heal the sick, to cast out devils, to achieve wonders out of Christ's poverty, to experience the thrilling joy of religion in the ever-abiding Divine Presence, and witness the marvels of faith in the conquering of the world? How is it we are no longer able to communicate the secrets to the suffering world which are able to transmute the people's want into God's plenty, and attract and hold the hearts of men with the joys of the Vision Splendid? Why is it that hope has given way to resignation, that the preaching of forgiveness has been dwarfed by the insistence upon penalty, that distinct evils in the physical sphere are attributed to God and, because of that, held up to religious estimation as good; the day of miracles is regarded as belonging to a far distant past, the answering of prayer looked upon as the exception instead of the rule, and the old melody of joy in religion exchanged for the wail of despair in an interpretation of 'Thy will be done' that is only associated with human calamity? The reply is as simple as, to the thoughtful person, it is obvious: we have lost knowledge of a living, vital, conquering faith that is rooted in God Himself, and have satisfied the hunger of human sense by placing trust in the things of the earth which we see and touch, and in so doing lost the power spiritually to achieve.

"Now we can only approach, in the hope of a day of better things, the great practical and intellectual problems of our times from the standpoint of faith's recovery, for it is only in their relationship to faith they can be viewed intelligently by the Christian. And it will be found that at the root of all our difficulties and all our negligences--so many of them unconscious--and as the cause of our vain expediencies and attempts to justify the corporate spiritual situation, is the absence of vital faith and a ***whole*** obedience to which God alone has conditioned results. We need sorely to reconsider what faith really is, and when we have recovered in some measure that knowledge of it in experience, which declared its unspeakable worth in the early Church and in later periods of ecclesiastical history which stand out before all others, we shall look back upon our past distrust of God and His promises with shame and wonderment, and proceed to revise our cataloguing of spiritual values and degrees of sin. For the really destructive thing, ***before all others,*** is a weakened faith that compromises in a half obedience to Christ and a search for earthly props. The work of Satan has even been the prompting of distrust of God in the human family, just as the work of redemption means so largely the re-establishing of it in the Person of Jesus Christ. From the first temptation of man to the present moment, all the forces of evil have concentrated upon breaking man's trust in God and His promises; every sin has had that as its ultimate end, and every disaster, ill and trial, in the world and individual life, is subtly presented by the enemy of God and man (knowing our haziness of vision), so as to place the appearances against the Creator in a blind disregard for the created; just as in the life of the Incarnate Son all the great power of the forces of darkness were brought to bear unsuccessfully upon the snapping of His faith in His Father--from the time He was tempted to believe Himself forgotten, when hungering and physically reduced in the wilderness after His long fast, until the dreadful cry of dereliction from the Cross at the very end.

"The call for reformation today, then, is to the doing of things left undone, the search for and recovery of almost lost spiritual powers that alone lastingly can achieve for God and hasten man's salvation. And this requires the venture and daring that breaks from the world, withdraws from compromise, and that, rightly estimating the character and attitude of God, refuses longer to believe Him the author of evils we resignedly accept today by calling them good; and instead, claims the powers of the Divine promises for the utter destruction of the world's ills by a strict dependence upon spiritual forces and weapons for the accomplishment of results. Above all, this means a change and reform in corporate conduct as the end of repentance, for the present almost total disregard of the laws and principles of Christian living as given in the Sermon on the Mount."

These are hard sayings and strong doctrine, but will any one say they are not true? The weakening of religion, with the consequent decline of civilization, is ultimately to be traced back to **organized** religion, not to religion itself, and still less to any inherent defects in Christianity. Where organized religion has failed it deserved to fail, because it countenanced disunion, forsook the saving sacraments, and finally compromised with worldliness and materialism. With each one of these false ventures faith began to weaken amongst the mass of people until at last this, which can always save, and alone can save, ceased to have either the power or the will to force the organism to conform to the spirit. If we have indeed accomplished the depth of our fall, then the time is at hand when we may hope and pray for a new outpouring of divine grace that will bring recovery.

There are wide evidences that men earnestly desire this. I have already spoken of the great corporate movements towards unity, and these mean much even though they may at present take on something of the quality of mechanism instead of depending on the individual and the grace of God working in him. The "World Conference on Faith and Order," the just effected federation of the Presbyterians, Methodists and Congregationalists in Canada, above all the eirenic manifesto of the Bishops at the last Lambeth Conference, all indicate a new spirit working potently in the souls of men. Concrete results are not as yet conspicuous, but the spirit is there and a beginning has been made. Even more significant is the wide testimony to the need for definite, concrete and pervasive religion that is daily given by men whose names have hitherto been quite dissociated from matters of this kind; scientists, educators, men of business and men of public life. It may be testimony in favour of some new invention, some synthetic product of curious and abnormal ingredients; as a matter of fact it frequently is, and we confront such remarkable products as Mr. Wells has given us, for example. The significant thing, however, is the fact of the desire and the avowal; if we have this I think we may leave it to God to see that the desire is satisfied in the end by heavenly food and not by the nostrums of ingenuity. For the same reason we may look without dismay on certain novel phenomena of the moment. In their divergence from "the Faith once delivered to the Saints" and left in the keeping of the Church Christ founded as a living and eternal organism through which His Spirit would work forever, they are wrong and therefore they cannot endure, but each testifies to the passionate desire in man for religion as a reality, and no one of them comes into existence except as the result of desperate action by men to recover something that had been taken from them and that their souls needed, and would have at any cost. Each one of these strange manifestations is a reaction from some old error that had become established belief or custom. No one who holds to historic Christianity is interested in them, but those who have found religion intellectualized beyond endurance and transformed either by materialism or rationalism, seek for the mysticism they know to be a reality (to employ a paradox) in the ultra mysticism of Oriental cults; those who revolt against the exaggeration of evil and its exaltation to eminence that rivals that of God Himself, which is the legacy of one powerful movement in the Reformation, rush to the other extreme and deny the existence of evil and even the reality of matter, while spiritism, the most insidious, perilous and fatal of all the spiritual temptations that beset the world at this time, gains as its adherents those who have been deprived of the Catholic belief in the Communion of Saints and have been forbidden to pray for the dead or to ask for their prayers and intercessions.

However strange and erroneous the actual manifestation, there is no question as to the reality and prevalence of the desire for the recovery of spiritual power through the channels of religion. It shows itself, as it should, first of all in the individual, and it is only recently that organized religion, Catholic or Protestant, has begun to show a sympathetic consciousness and to take the first hesitant steps towards meeting the demand. Because of this the seekers for reality have been left unshepherded and have wandered off into strange wildernesses. The call is now to the churches, to organized religion, and if the call is heeded our troubles are well on the road to an end. If the old way of jealousy, hatred and fear is maintained, then humanly speaking, our case is hopeless. If the older way of brotherhood, charity and loving-kindness is followed the future is secure in the Great Peace. Nothing is wrong that leads men to Christ, and this is true from the Salvation Army at one end of the scale to the Seven Sacraments of Catholicity at the other. The world demands now not denial but affirmation, not protest and division but the ringing "Credo" of Catholic unity.

VIII
PERSONAL RESPONSIBILITY

Not by might, nor by power, but by My Spirit, saith the Lord of Hosts.

We have tried to approach each subject in this course of lectures in the spirit of peace, and the greatest contributory factor in the achieving of the Great Peace is the individual himself, on whom, humanly speaking, rests the final responsibility. "Not by might, nor by power, but by My Spirit, saith the Lord of Hosts." Not by majestical engines and curious devices and mass-action, nor yet by an imposed human authority enforced by arms and the law, but by the Holy Spirit of God working through the individual soul and compelling the individual will. Peace is one of the promised fruits of the Holy Spirit, and like the others is manifested through human lives; therefore on us rests the preeminent responsibility of showing forth in ourselves, first of all, those things we desire for others and for society.

We have experienced the Great War, we endure its aftermath, and amidst the perils and dangers that follow both there is none greater than that which attaches to exterior war, viz., that the attention of both combatants is focussed on the faults and the weaknesses and the crimes of the opponent, with the result that both become destructive critics rather than constructive examples. Chesterton rightly says, "What is wrong with the critic is that he does not criticise himself * * * rather he identifies himself with the ideal." Seeing evil in others and flattering one's self is the antithesis of the spirit that would lead to the Great Peace, for in that spirit the field of warfare is transferred from the external to the internal, and the interior contest, which alone establishes lasting results, necessitates a recognition of our own error and the need of amendment of our own life.

If our modern devices have failed; if the things we invented with a high heart and high hope, in government, industry, society, education, philosophy have in the end brought disappointment, disillusionment, even despair, it is less because of their inherent defects than because the individual failed, and himself ceased to act as the sufficient channel for the divine power which alone energizes our weak little engines and which acts through the individual alone. There is no better demonstration of this essential part played by the personal life of man than the fact that God, for the redemption of the world, took on human form and became one Man amongst many men. There is no better demonstration of the fact that it is through the personal lives of individuals that the Great Peace is to be achieved, both directly and indirectly, than the fact that peace, the gift of the Holy Spirit, was promised to the individual man, by Christ Himself, as the legacy he left to his disciples after His Resurrection and Ascension. Since then the world has been under the dispensation of the Holy Spirit, the "Guide and Comforter" that was promised, even though it has blindly and from time to time rejected the guidance and therefore known not the comfort. The Old Law of "Thou shalt not" was followed by the New Law of "Thou shalt," and this in turn by the law of the third Person of the Trinity which does not supersede the dispensations of the Father and of the Son, but fulfills them in that it affords the spiritual power, if we will, to abide by the inhibitions and to carry out the commands.

Our search is for peace, the Great Peace, "the Peace of God which passeth all understanding," and we shall achieve this for ourselves and for the world only through ourselves as individuals, and so for the society of which we are a part, and in so far as we bring ourselves into contact with the Spirit of God. There is deep significance in the fact that the first time Christ used the salutation "Peace be unto you," was after His resurrection. It would seem that this special gift of the Holy Spirit had to be withheld from man until after the human life of God the Son had been brought to an end in accomplishment, for He says "Peace I leave with you, My peace I give unto you: not as the world giveth give I unto you. Let not your heart be troubled, neither let it be afraid." "It is expedient for you that I go away; for if I go not away, the Comforter will not come unto you: but if I depart I will send Him unto you. When He, the Spirit of Truth, is come, He will guide you into all truth."

"Ye shall receive power after that the Holy Ghost is come upon you."

It is the spirit that quickeneth. After God had revealed the Law and given to us the great redeeming and atoning Life, He saw that we had need of a further manifestation before we should be able to keep the law and live the life. Therefore the Holy Spirit was sent to quicken us and give us power to do what we had both heard and seen. Today we accept the moral law, we recognize the perfection of Chirst's life, but we need to be reminded again that the power to be "sons of God" is present with us if we will but use it. As this power is a spirit it can only be apprehended spiritually; when our minds and hearts are set on material things, even on good material things, the "still small voice" of the spirit remains unheard: but if we listen first to that inward voice and then use the means of grace afforded us, we are enabled to lift up our hearts and minds to the Creator and then to use in His service all the material universe which is also His creation. We can not get a right philosophy by working for right philosophy, but only by living in the right relationship as individuals: then as a by-product of religion a right philosophy will come. We can not get a right industrial system by searching for a right industrial system, but if we show forth in our lives the Christian virtues, a right industrial system will come as one of the by-products of religion. So with each one of our so-called "problems." Life rightly lived has no problems. This is a hard saying for an intellectual age whose temptation is to trust in its own power rather than in the power of God, but "except ye become as little children" and walk by faith and not by sight the Kingdom of God is withheld. A soldier who suffered in the late war, and out of his suffering found peace, says, "Christ's hardest work is to teach the wise: Those who are entrusted with authority and responsibility will be the least prepared to make the venture of the Spirit, however much they may believe in it. They are sacrificing least now: they will have to sacrifice most when the Spirit comes. They have so much to unlearn: children and working men have so little. The whole of our world today is rooted and grounded in intellect. Our machinery, our institutions, our great systems, the entire body of enterprise is governed by brains. It is this that will alter. Just behind intellect there is a vision that is purer, keener, more powerful than the vision of your eyes, than the hearing of your ears, than the touch of your hands. This world is being transformed into another which comes into being at our spiritual touch. The world needs something personal, something from the heart. It is sick to death with the cold machinery of the intellect. But before men see this they must change their view of life, they must **be born again.** The scientists, the historians and theologians, the philosophers, have made the universe too big. It is not a big place: it is very tiny. Life is so simple, really. Our wise men have made it so difficult, so ugly. It is only children who can see the risen Christ; children, perhaps, out of whom seven devils have been cast. The world needs not critics, but teachers, and children are waiting everywhere to teach, but men, shutting the windows of their souls, try rather to mould these little ones to fit into the vacant spaces of their own stupid world. Are not children the true artists? They won't tolerate anything but Beauty. They see Beauty everywhere, not because it is there, but because they want it there. Everything they touch turns into something far more precious than gold: every word they utter is a song of praise. You are almost in heaven every time you look into the eyes of a child." Remember, please, these are the words of a man who has faced the horrible realities of modern warfare, and so do not dismiss them as mere poetry, or with Nicodemus' question, "How can a man be born again?", but listen to a modern interpretation of the answer to that question:--("The Life Indeed.") "We must be born again even to see the spiritual kingdom, must be born of water and the spirit to enter its gates at all. So to his little audience of disciples Our Lord says it is not an affair of legislation, of discovery, of which men say, 'Lo here, lo there! but the kingdom of heaven is **within you.** Why a second birth? This is a second birth because it must needs supervene at a point where two elements can work together, the element of an appealing, vitalizing spirit from the unseen and the element of free human choice. Being of the spirit, it is the birth into freedom: it is the soul emerging from its prison into the open air of liberty and light and life." Note the element of free choice. Our first birth is outside our choice and the gifts are unconditioned; our second birth, when again we become as little children, demands our response to the Holy Spirit and our persevering cooperation with Him to make His influence effectual for ourselves and for the "communion of saints" and the corporate religion into which the Spirit also baptizes us. In a recent sermon a bishop of the Episcopal Church says, "This is the creed of the Church--the Divine Father and Forgiveness: the Divine Son and Redemption: the Divine Spirit and Abundant Life. Therefore the Church still insists upon the creation of moral rectitude and spiritual character as the end and purpose of religion, aye, as the basic problem underlying all questions relating to human life--social, industrial, civic, and political. The Church still preaches the gospel of the Grace of God, the obligation and blessing of worship, the meaning and virtue of the Christian Sacraments." Also "My brethren, we shall not be content to criticize and find fault with our own age and time, but rather we shall pray for the power to see within its questionings, unrest and discontent--aye, its recklessness and apparent failures--the strivings of the Spirit of God. But each man has to voice for himself the conviction of the reality of the spiritual order and the spiritual life. Therefore, let us believe in and practice the worship of God, 'praying always' as St. Paul says, 'with all prayer and supplication in the Spirit,' or as St. Jude says, 'building up yourselves on your most holy faith, praying in the Holy Spirit.'"

Let us accept this suggestion and try to find in the unrest of our own time evidences of "the strivings of the Spirit of God," waiting our perception and response. The soldier of the Great War, having faced death and imprisonment and suffering in many forms says, "compared with the depth of good in the world the evil is shallow." The first evidence of good in our own day is the almost universal discontent with evils and the desire to find a better way. The humility which recognizes that so widespread a condition cannot be the fault of any one nation or group but is rather the responsibility of each one of us, is cause for hope. Some of us believe that war can breed only war, hatred only hatred; that governments cannot make peace, but can only cause cessation of open hostilities, and that the real peace, the Great Peace, must await the action of the Spirit. This Spirit, of love and forgiveness, breeds love and forgiveness, indeed is far more potent than the spirit of hate. Because of this very strength and potency its evidences are not so immediately apparent, but they are deeper-rooted. Perhaps in this material sphere we human beings must see, and to a certain extent experience, hate, before we can really know love, and consciously and freely choose it. When that choice is made, when we, knowing all that hate and evil and malice can accomplish, yet deliberately choose to love our enemies, we have slain the Adversary and made hate and evil powerless. Of course we have not power of ourselves to do this but only through the grace of God. When we try God's way, not waiting for the other person to reform or to be generous or to speak gently or to forgive, then and only then do we deserve the name of Christians; then and only then are we walking in love; then and only then are we really praying effectually "Thy Kingdom come, Thy will be done on earth as it is in Heaven." We have tried the way of the world, the way of reprisals, the way of distrust, and, thank God, we are none of us satisfied with the results. Perhaps now we may be ready to try the way of God by making the great adventure of faith, each one in his own person; faith in himself and faith in the future. The way of the world has bred fear that has issue in hate, and hate that has issue in fear; but the better way, that of faith, breeds trust that has issue in fellowship, and fellowship that has issue in trust. There is no problem of labour, of politics, of society that is insoluble if once it is approached in the spirit of faith and fellowship and trust, but none of these is susceptible of solution where the controlling motives are hate, distrust and fear. The modern policy of centralization and segregation has resulted in dealing with men as groups and not as individuals. When, for example, iron-bound cults (they are no less than this) meet as "capital" and as "labour," both merge the individuality of their members in a thing which has no real or necessary existence but is an artificial creation of thought operating under the dominion of ephemeral, almost accidental conditions. As a member of an "interest" or a cult, where humanity and personality are, so to speak, "in commission," a man does not hesitate to do those things he would never think of doing for himself, knowing them to be selfish, cruel, unjust and uncharitable. A case in point--if we need one, which is hardly probable since they are of daily occurrence--is the pending contest between the mine operators and mine workers in Great Britain, where both parties, with Government thrown in, are guilty of maintaining theories and perpetrating acts for which an individual would be, even now, excoriated and outlawed. The Irish imbroglio is another instance of the same kind.

In a personal letter from a consulting engineer who has had unusual opportunities, by reason of his official position, to come closely in contact with the conditions governing industry and finance both in America and Europe since the war, I find this illuminating statement of a matured judgment. "As a practical matter, and facing the issue, I would preach the practice of de-centralization in government and business which will in time develop the individual and accomplish the desired end. * * * Decentralization should be carried to such an extent that the units of business would be of such size that the head could again have a personal relation with each individual associated with him. * * * With the personal relation again established, unionism as at present practiced would again be unnecessary, and the unions would become once more guilds for the development and advancement of the individual." It is this nullification of the human element, of the person as such, the introduction of the gross aggregate with its artificial corporate quality, and the attempt to establish a correspondence between these unnatural things, the whole being intensified by the emotions of fear, distrust and hate, which produces the contemporary insistence on "rights" and the rank injustice, cruelty and disorder that follow the blind contest. To quote again from the soldier who achieved illumination through the recent war, "My friends, there is no protection of rights in heaven. When we speak of rights we are blinded by the light of this world of rule and order and intellectual conceits. It is not justice we need, it is mercy."

If we honestly endeavour to bring about something more nearly approaching the Kingdom of God on earth, we should do well to achieve a little more of the quality of child-like trust which knows that through the petition to father or mother, or to a guardian angel, or directly to God, the result will surely follow. We long passionately to see a good, *our* good as we see it, accepted here and now, but whatever we offer, no mater how righteous or how salutary, is but a small part of the great good, a limited and partial showing forth of only one element, while the final and comprehensive good is the result of many contributions, and in the end is not ours, but God's, and by His overruling providence it may look very unlike what we had predetermined and anticipated. Moreover, the condition even of our own small good becoming effective, is ***faith,*** and neither sight nor action. There is a faith that can move mountains, and it is faith in fellowship, in the underlying, indestructible good in man, above all in the desire and the intent of God to deal mercifully with us and beyond the dictates of justice and the claims of our own deserts. When we know and accept this power of faith, placing it above the efficiency of our own feeble works, then indeed we may become the patient, hopeful, joyful and faithful Christians we were intended to be, and therefore the creators of the spirit of peace. Nothing permanent can be achieved except in cooeperation with God; any work of man alone (or of the devil) has in it the seed of decay and must perish, This knowledge relieves us of the gloomy responsibility of destroying or trying to destroy every evil thing we see or think we see. If it is really evil it is already dying unless nourished by evil within ourselves. Here is a Buddhist legend which has a lesson for each of us--"The watcher in the shrine of Buddha rushed in to the Holy Fathers one morning with tidings of a horrible demon who had usurped the throne of our Lord Buddha. The Fathers ran to the throne room, each one more infuriated than the other, and declaimed against the insolence of the demon, who grew huger and more hideous at every angry word that hurtled through the air. At last arrived the oldest and most saintly of the monks and threw himself on his knees before the demon and said, "We thank thee, O Master, for teaching us how much anger and wrath and jealousy was still hidden in our hearts." At every word he said, the demon grew smaller and smaller and at last vanished. He was am Anger-Eating Demon, and anger-rousing words and even thoughts of ill-feeling nourished him.

The belief that in comparison with the depth of good in the world the evil is shallow may also be expressed in the statement that God is Lord of Eternity while the devil is prince only of this world. As this evil spirit has power, and as a part of this power is the ability to appear as an angel of light, so to deceive us, we are bound by self-examination, constantly indulged in, to scrutinize those things, so common in our own lives we do not notice them, which may be but the illusions of this spirit of darkness showing as a fictitious spirit of light: Hurry and carelessness both in thought and in action; snap-judgment at short range; compromise with the spirit of the time in the interest of "good business," "practical considerations" or "sound policy"; worship of the doctrine of "get results," acceptance of the horrible principle: that it is every man's business to "sell" something to another, from a patent medicine or "gilt edged" bonds to a new philosophy or an old religion; the estimating of values by size, number, cost. It is common parlance among Christian people to speak of what a man "is worth" meaning how much money he has. We speak of a man's "making a living" meaning only how much money he makes, when by making only money he would be killing his living. Do we not speak of the call of a missionary from an unshepherded flock to a large city parish as a call to "a wider sphere of usefulness"? When you or I conceive of any piece of work as "important" is it not because it involves either great numbers or great sums of money? Then we hear much today of the need for leaders. The need could not be exaggerated, but does not this lack exist, in part, because we have forgot that the Christian's first duty is to be a follower, and that only from amongst real followers can God (not man, least of all the man himself) raise up a leader? These are small matters, you may say, but "straws show which way the wind blows," and the spirit, like the wind, manifests itself first in small matters. Every life is made up largely of small things, "the little, nameless unremembered acts of kindness and of love" which some one has called "the noblest portion of a good man's life."

With this brief glance at some of the possible manifestations of the spirit of evil which we believe to be temporary and therefore of secondary importance only, let us consider some of the requisites of the Christian life as exemplified in the life of Christ, especially those of which we need to be reminded today. We have already spoken of that child-likeness which takes the faith simply and applies it to the common things of daily life--Christ's life of ministry, of good works (which was, in proportion to the time given to preparation for activity and preaching, of very short duration), full of injunctions to those who were with him to "tell no man"; therefore the good works which are done "in His likeness" must not be done in public. If we are "seen of men," verily we have our reward. Christ's life ended in apparent failure, in ignominious death on the cross. The world worships today's success and immediate publicity, the Christian, to be worthy of his Lord, must accept apparent failure and must offer his best work in secret: "And my Father which seeth in secret, shall reward thee openly." A touching poem of Francis Thompson's pictures the marveling of a soul on his rewards in Paradise which, in his humility, he thinks undeserved. The man asks of God:

> O when did I give Thee drink erewhile,
> Or when embrace Thine unseen feet?
> What gifts Thee give for my Lord Christ's smile,
> Who am a guest here most unmeet?
> and is answered
>
> When thou kissedest thy wife and children sweet
> (Their eyes are fair in my sight as thine)
> I felt the embraces on My feet.
> (Lovely their locks in thy sight and Mine.)

A necessary reminder of the fact that for each of us, charity, which is love, begins at home, and that we love and serve God best in His holy human relationships--if we love not our brother whom we have seen how can we love God whom we have not seen?

Again, the individual Christian life must, like its Great Original, suffer for others. When we suffer as a result of our own wrongdoing we are but meeting our just reward; but if patiently and humbly and voluntarily we bear pain, even unto death, for others, we are transcending justice, the pagan law, and exemplifying mercy, the Christian virtue. No sensitive soul in this generation, conscious of the sacrifice of the millions of young lives who "stormed Heaven" in their willingness to die that others might live, can doubt this. The essence of love is sacrifice; voluntary, nay eager sacrifice. Before our Blessed Lord died He was mocked and ridiculed, He suffered physical hardship, falling under the weight of the cross, and He was lifted up, crucified, to suffer the ignominious death of a felon. He was made a spectacle for the jests and laughter of the multitude. In our own time and amongst ourselves, except for periods of war, there is little necessity for physical suffering for our faith, but the need to endure ridicule is as great as ever, perhaps even greater because of the absence of physical suffering. Since we are trying to apply these things in small and simple ways to the individual life let us each one consider how much moral courage it takes to defend Christian virtues when they are sneered at under the guise of "jokes." Let us exercise charity by not quoting instances, but let us be watchful of our laughter and our fellowship, which are both gifts of God, and see that we do not confuse pagan pleasure with Christian joy, the evil sneer with the tender recognition of the absurd in ourselves and in others. It is Mr. Chesterton again who points out the fact that the pagan virtues of justice and the like which he calls the "sad virtues" were superseded, when the great Christian revelation came, by the "gay and exuberant virtues," the virtues of grace, faith, hope and charity; and who says, "the pagan virtues are the reasonable virtues, and the Christian virtues of faith, hope and charity are in their essence as unreasonable as they can be. Charity means pardoning what is unpardonable or it is no virtue at all. Hope means hoping when things are hopeless or it is no virtue at all. And faith means believing the incredible or it is no virtue at all." If you say this is a paradox I reply: it must be so, since it requires faith to accept a paradox. The realm of reason is the one in which we walk by sight, and of this fact our age in its pride of intellect has need to be reminded.

If Christ be not the Son of God, and His revelation of the "faith once delivered" be not the divine and final guide, fulfilling, completing and at the same time reversing every other ethic, religion and moral code, then these things be indeed foolishness, for there is no explaining them on the ground of logic or philosophy. But if, by the gift of grace, we have faith, we remember "I thank Thee, Father, that Thou hast hid these things from the wise and prudent, and has revealed them unto babes: even so, Father, for so it seemed good in Thy sight."

Again, and if as persons we are to grow in relationship to a personal God, we must both speak and listen to our Father; in other words we must use the great dynamic of prayer. "More things are wrought by prayer than this world dreams of." We are told that one of the requisites of the really good talker is to be a good listener; the apparently good talker is in reality a monologuist. In our prayer-life today do we recognize sufficiently the need for *listening* to God? We are perhaps ready enough to ask for blessings and mercies, but that is only a part of the full life of prayer which must include also thanksgiving, lifting of the heart and mind, and quiet listening or interior prayer. There was an age in the world when this interior prayer was so much more joyful and natural a thing than the world of matter that it had to be taught "to labour is to pray." Today, when we accept the necessity of labour, and even worship activity for its own sake, do we not need to be reminded that to pray is to labour? If you doubt this, try to make that concentrated form of prayer known as meditation, out of which springs a resolve and determination to do better; try to do this faithfully for fifteen minutes a day and it may prove the hardest work you have ever undertaken. A great servant of God has said, "I believe no soul can be lost which faithfully practices meditation for fifteen minutes a day." Nor must we forget that in this work of prayer we are companioned by the Holy Spirit, the Peace-maker, Who maketh intercession for us "with groanings which can not be uttered" and "Who leads us ever gently but surely into that closer communion with God whose result is life more abundant." After prayer it is easier to realize that "to be spiritually minded is life and peace"; it is easier to obey the injunction "And grieve not the Holy Spirit of God whereby ye are sealed unto the day of redemption. Let all bitterness, and wrath, and anger, and clamour, and evil speaking be put away from you, with all malice, and be ye kind one to another, tender-hearted, forgiving one another, even as God, for Christ's sake, hath forgiven you." And for those that seek after peace it must be *all* wrath, *all* anger and *all* evil speaking which are put away: This leaves no room for what the world calls "just wrath" "righteous anger," or speaking evil of evil doers. Let us call to mind the incident in the early life of St. John, afterwards the great disciple of love, when he wanted to call down wrath on the wicked inhabitants of a city and was rebuked by Our Lord who said, "Ye know not in what spirit ye speak." After love had supplanted wrath, and the good spirit had taken the place of the evil in St. John's heart, he was sent to convert the people he would have destroyed. Yes, it is the spirit that matters, the wrath that is wrong and that must be put away before we can love God or our neighbour as ourself, for the fruit of the Spirit is love, joy, peace, long suffering, gentleness, goodness, faith, meekness, temperance.

When we understand that the object of life and of education is the creation of a spirit and not the doing of things, we are freed from the tyranny of results in this world as a final test and come to realize that judgment belongs only to God Who as a Spirit judges the effort.

Of course this does not mean that we are freed from the moral law, that certain evil things in ourselves and in others are not always the results of an evil spirit, but rather that in addition to avoiding and shunning those things which are obviously evil, we must with equal care avoid doing even good things in a bad spirit. The commandments still stand, the moral law is abated not one jot, but in Christianity and in Christianity alone are we given power to fulfill the law and to add the new commandment, the summing up of them all, of love to God and man. No human soul comes into the world without some desire to be good, because each human soul is a child of God. To each one, not blinded by pride (and surely it should be easy in these days to be humble) comes, sooner or later, the realization of his own inability of himself to do what he would, the need for a power outside himself, the power which is available and of which we have heard "I am come that ye might have life and more abundantly." Let us examine how the apostles set about living this abundant life. In Dr. Genung's "The Life Indeed" we read, "One and all they made it a matter of the spirit that is the man, but the spirit they recognized was not an abstraction, or a theory, but a present Person and helper who was witnessing with their spirits. St. John makes the matter equally definite: 'The Son of God,' he says, 'was manifest that he might destroy the works of the Devil,' and St. Paul, mindful of the inner subtleties of the conflict, warns his readers that Satan has changed his tactics and has transformed himself into an angel of light. I am not sure that we have gained greatly by letting our notions of spiritual life grow dim and abstract. Perhaps for this very reason the rebellious, negative, designing spirit that is so prone to invade the hearts of us all is the more free to gain a foot-hold and go about controlling the tone of our life. There is real advantage in bringing the large issues of life to a point where not only our mind but, as it were, our senses, can lay hold on them. It is the impulse of simple-minded men like those early disciples, and if we continue straight-seeing we do not outgrow it. What makes these views of life so deep is not that they are less simple than those of others, but that they are more simple. To St. John the reality that has come to win the world is not the promise of salvation, or prophecy of an eventual life eternal, but just life without modification or limitation, life absolute, full-orbed, pulsating through worlds seen and unseen alike. 'I am the Life,' he makes Christ say, not, 'I am working to secure it.' St. John it is who preserves to us that conception of eating the Flesh and drinking the Blood of the Son of Man. No philosopher in the world, we may roundly say, would ever have put it so, and yet how effectually is thus revealed what it means to get the power of the new life thoroughly incorporated with our blood and breath. He it is who identifies the most inner values of life with the simplest acts and experiences, reducing it to terms of eating bread and drinking water, and walking in daylight, and bearing fruit like the branches of a vine and following like sheep the voice of a shepherd, and entering a door and finding pasture."

Let us cease trying materialistic and intellectual means for supplying the power to live the spiritual life and let us each one establish the needful relationship with the true source of power. May our time not be likened to the Oriental traveler, who, appreciating the convenience and force of electricity as seen in a room he occupied, fitted his palace, on his return, with a set of elaborate fixtures and was surprised to find no illumination therefrom! We are torches who can not shine in themselves, but who, when connected with the great central Source of Power, the Blessed Trinity in its three glorious manifestations, can show forth the light of the world. Christians should be torch bearers, and the true torch bearer lights not his own path so much as the path of those who come after him. And this brings us to the fundamental reason for personal responsibility. Our motive in seeking personal righteousness it not, as might hastily be thought, because of a selfish desire to save our own souls, or to withdraw either here or hereafter from other souls, but for "their sakes" to sanctify ourselves; for the lives we live today create the spiritual atmosphere of tomorrow.

From Spain come the following suggestive thoughts in regard to the value of the person. "The individual is the real purpose of the universe. We may seek the hero of our thought in no philosopher who lived in flesh and blood, but in a being of fiction and of action, more real than all the philosophers. He is Don Quixote. One cannot say of Don Quixote that he was strictly idealistic. He did not fight for ideas: he was of the spirit and he fought for the spirit. Quixotism is a madness descended from the madness of the cross; therefore it is despised by reason; Don Quixote will not resign himself to either the world or its truth, to science or logic, to art or aesthetics, to morals or ethics. And what did he leave behind him? one may ask. I reply that he left himself, and that a man, a man living and immortal, is worth all theories and all philosophies. Other countries have left us institutions and books: Spain has left soul. St. Theresa is worth all institutions whatever, or any 'Critique of Pure Reason.'"

Yes, this is I think the lesson we have to learn, now at this turning point in history with the epoch of intellect crumbling about our ears, and the great World's Fair of multiplied, ingenious mechanisms we have called "modern civilization" at a point of practical bankruptcy. It is the spirit that counts, the soul of "man living and immortal," and only through our own living, and the spiritual force that we can command, and through ourselves apply, shall we be able to compass that social regeneration that is the only alternative to social degeneration and catastrophe. The man who does not live his belief is powerless to redeem or to create, though he were a Solon, a Charlemagne, a Napoleon or a Washington; the man who lives his belief, even if he is a mill-hand in Fall River, is contributing something of energizing force to the task of re-creation. "Not by might, nor by power, but by my Spirit, saith the Lord of Hosts."

Fantastic and paradoxical as it may seem to link together Don Quixote and St. Theresa, I am not sure that we could do better than to accept them as models. The loud laughter of an age of intellectual ribaldry and self-conceit dies away and the gaunt figure of the last of the Crusaders still stands before us heroic in his childlike refusal of compromise, his burning compassion, his deafness to ridicule. In a sense we must all be ready to accept the jeering and the scorn that were poured out on the Knight of La Mancha, if like him we are to fight, even foolishly, for the things that are worth fighting for--either that they may be destroyed, or restored. And with St. Theresa we must be willing to endure obloquy, suspicion, malice, if like her we live in faith, subjecting our will to the divine will, and then sparing nothing of ourselves in the labour of saving the world for God in the twentieth century as St. Theresa laboured to save it in the sixteenth century.

The call today is for personal service through the right living that follows the discovery of a right relationship to God. Not a campaign but a crusade; and the figures of St. Louis and St. Francis and St. Theresa, together with all the Knights and Crusaders of Christendom, rise up before us to point the way. We would find the Great Peace, the world would find the Great Peace also, but

The way is all so very plain
That we may lose the way.

We have been told: "Seek ye first the Kingdom of God and His righteousness, and all these things shall be added unto you, for your Heavenly Father knoweth ye have need of these things." If we go forth on this new and knightly quest--quest indeed in these latter days, for the Holy Grail, lost long since and hidden away from men--we may, by the grace of God, achieve. Then, "suddenly, in the twinkling of an eye," and before we are aware, for "the Kingdom of God cometh not with watching," we and even the world, shall find that we have compassed the Great Peace, and if we do not live to see it, yet in our "certain hope" we shall know that it will come, if not in our time, yet in God's good time; if not in our way, yet in His more perfect way.

In these lectures I have from time to time, and perhaps beyond your patience, criticised and condemned many of those concrete institutions which form the working mechanism of life, even suggesting possible substitutes. In ending I would say as in beginning; this is not because salvation may be found through any device, however perfect, but because this itself, by reason of its excellence on the one hand or its depravity on the other, is, under the law of life, contributory to the operation of the divine spirit (which is the sole effective energy) or a deterrent. I have tried at long last to gather up this diffuse argument for the supremacy of spiritual force as it works through the individual, and to place it before you in this concluding lecture. Perhaps I can best emphasize my point thus.

The evil of the institutions which now hold back the progress that must be made towards social recovery and the Great Peace, is far less the quality of wrongness in themselves and the ill influence they put in operation, than it is the revelation they make of personal character. It is not so much that newspapers are what they are as that there should be men who are pleased and content to make them this, in apparently honest ignorance of what they are doing, and that there should be others in sufficient number to make them profitable business propositions by giving them their appreciation and support. It is not so much that government should be what it is as that character should have so far degenerated in the working majority of citizens that these qualities should show themselves as a fixed condition, and that there should be no body of men of numerical distinction, who regard the situation with sentiments much more active than those of indifference and amused toleration. It is not so much that the industrial situation should be what it is, as that there should be on both sides moral wrong, and that this condition could not have come about, nor could it still be maintained, except through character degeneration in the individual. It is not so much that many forms of religion are what they are, as it is that they should progressively have become this through their exponents and adherents, and that there should be so many who are still willing to defend them in this case.

Every ill thing reveals through its very quality the defects of the individual man, and as upon him must rest the responsibilities for the fault, so on him must be placed the responsibility for the recovery. The failures we have recorded, the false gods we have raised up in idolatry, even the Great War itself, are revelations of failure in personal and individual character. We may recognize this, but recognition is not enough. We may found societies and committees and write books and deliver lectures, but corporate action is not enough, nor intellectual assent. There is but one way that is right, sufficient and effective, and that is the right living of each individual, which is the incarnation and operation of faith by the grace of God.

It is my desire to close this course of lectures not with my own words but with those of one of the great personalities revealed by the war. First, however, I wish to say this. If there is any thought or word in what I have said that seems to you true, then I ask you to use it not as a matter for discussion but as an impulse toward personal action. If there is anything that is of the nature of explicit error, then I pray that the Spirit of Truth may make deaf your ears that you hear not, and blot out of your memory the record of what I have said. If there is anything that is not consonant with the Christian religion, as this has been revealed to the world and as it is guarded and interpreted by the Church to which these powers were committed, then I retract and disavow it explicitly and ***ex animo.***

There are two great spiritual figures that have been revealed to us through the Great War: Cardinal Mercier, the great confessor, who held aloft the standard of spiritual glory through the war itself, and Bishop Nicholai of Serbia who has testified to eternal truth and righteousness in the wilderness the war has brought to pass. It is with his inspired words that I will make an ending of the things I have been impelled to say.

"Christ is merciful, but at last He comes as the Judge. *** He comes now not to preside in the churches only but to be in your homes, in your shops, to be everywhere with you. He wants to be first; He has become last in Europe, *** Civilization passes like the winds, but the soul remains. Christianization is the only good and constructive civilization. Americanization without Christianization means Bolshevism. Europe is suffering today for her sins. Christ has forgiven seventy times seven, and now it seems that He is the Judge, turning away, rejected, leaving Europe and going through the gate of Serbia to Asia. Pray for us. *** Send us not your gold and silver for food so much as send us converted men. Convert your politicians, your members of the press, your journalists, to preach Christ.

"Christ is choosing the perfect stones, the marble of all the churches, to complete His mystical body in Heaven. He thinks only of one Church, made from those true to Him of all the churches here. Civilizations are moving pictures, made by man. Without God they perish. The soul, the spirit, lives. The war is not against externals; the war is against ourselves."

www.bookjungle.com *email: sales@bookjungle.com fax: 630-214-0564 mail: Book Jungle PO Box 2226 Champaign, IL 61825*

The Codes Of Hammurabi And Moses
W. W. Davies

QTY

The discovery of the Hammurabi Code is one of the greatest achievements of archaeology, and is of paramount interest, not only to the student of the Bible, but also to all those interested in ancient history...

Religion   ISBN: *1-59462-338-4*   Pages:132
MSRP $12.95

The Theory of Moral Sentiments
Adam Smith

QTY

This work from 1749. contains original theories of conscience amd moral judgment and it is the foundation for systemof morals.

Philosophy ISBN: *1-59462-777-0*   Pages:536
MSRP $19.95

Jessica's First Prayer
Hesba Stretton

QTY

In a screened and secluded corner of one of the many railway-bridges which span the streets of London there could be seen a few years ago, from five o'clock every morning until half past eight, a tidily set-out coffee-stall, consisting of a trestle and board, upon which stood two large tin cans, with a small fire of charcoal burning under each so as to keep the coffee boiling during the early hours of the morning when the work-people were thronging into the city on their way to their daily toil...

Childrens   ISBN: *1-59462-373-2*   Pages:84
MSRP $9.95

My Life and Work
Henry Ford

QTY

Henry Ford revolutionized the world with his implementation of mass production for the Model T automobile. Gain valuable business insight into his life and work with his own auto-biography... "We have only started on our development of our country we have not as yet, with all our talk of wonderful progress, done more than scratch the surface. The progress has been wonderful enough but..."

Biographies/   ISBN: *1-59462-198-5*   Pages:300
MSRP $21.95

www.bookjungle.com *email: sales@bookjungle.com fax: 630-214-0564 mail: Book Jungle PO Box 2226 Champaign, IL 61825*

The Art of Cross-Examination
Francis Wellman

QTY

I presume it is the experience of every author, after his first book is published upon an important subject, to be almost overwhelmed with a wealth of ideas and illustrations which could readily have been included in his book, and which to his own mind, at least, seem to make a second edition inevitable. Such certainly was the case with me; and when the first edition had reached its sixth impression in five months, I rejoiced to learn that it seemed to my publishers that the book had met with a sufficiently favorable reception to justify a second and considerably enlarged edition. ...

Reference   ISBN: *1-59462-647-2*   Pages:412 MSRP *$19.95*

On the Duty of Civil Disobedience
Henry David Thoreau

QTY

Thoreau wrote his famous essay, On the Duty of Civil Disobedience, as a protest against an unjust but popular war and the immoral but popular institution of slave-owning. He did more than write—he declined to pay his taxes, and was hauled off to gaol in consequence. Who can say how much this refusal of his hastened the end of the war and of slavery?

Law   ISBN: *1-59462-747-9*   Pages:48 MSRP *$7.45*

Dream Psychology Psychoanalysis for Beginners
Sigmund Freud

QTY

Sigmund Freud, born Sigismund Schlomo Freud (May 6, 1856 - September 23, 1939), was a Jewish-Austrian neurologist and psychiatrist who co-founded the psychoanalytic school of psychology. Freud is best known for his theories of the unconscious mind, especially involving the mechanism of repression; his redefinition of sexual desire as mobile and directed towards a wide variety of objects; and his therapeutic techniques, especially his understanding of transference in the therapeutic relationship and the presumed value of dreams as sources of insight into unconscious desires.

Psychology   ISBN: *1-59462-905-6*   Pages:196 MSRP *$15.45*

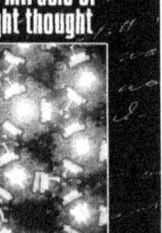

The Miracle of Right Thought
Orison Swett Marden

QTY

Believe with all of your heart that you will do what you were made to do. When the mind has once formed the habit of holding cheerful, happy, prosperous pictures, it will not be easy to form the opposite habit. It does not matter how improbable or how far away this realization may see, or how dark the prospects may be, if we visualize them as best we can, as vividly as possible, hold tenaciously to them and vigorously struggle to attain them, they will gradually become actualized, realized in the life. But a desire, a longing without endeavor, a yearning abandoned or held indifferently will vanish without realization.

Self Help   ISBN: *1-59462-644-8*   Pages:360 MSRP *$25.45* www.bookjungle.com email: sales@bookjungle.com fax: 630-214-0564 mail: Book Jungle PO Box 2226 Champaign, IL 61825

QTY

	Title	ISBN	Price
☐	**The Rosicrucian Cosmo-Conception Mystic Christianity** by *Max Heindel*	ISBN: 1-59462-188-8	$38.95

The Rosicrucian Cosmo-conception is not dogmatic, neither does it appeal to any other authority than the reason of the student. It is: not controversial, but is: sent forth in the, hope that it may help to clear...
New Age/Religion Pages 646

☐ **Abandonment To Divine Providence** by *Jean-Pierre de Caussade* ISBN: 1-59462-228-0 $25.95
"The Rev. Jean Pierre de Caussade was one of the most remarkable spiritual writers of the Society of Jesus in France in the 18th Century. His death took place at Toulouse in 1751. His works have gone through many editions and have been republished...
Inspirational/Religion Pages 400

☐ **Mental Chemistry** by *Charles Haanel* ISBN: 1-59462-192-6 $23.95
Mental Chemistry allows the change of material conditions by combining and appropriately utilizing the power of the mind. Much like applied chemistry creates something new and unique out of careful combinations of chemicals the mastery of mental chemistry...
New Age Pages 354

☐ **The Letters of Robert Browning and Elizabeth Barret Barrett 1845-1846 vol II** ISBN: 1-59462-193-4 $35.95
by *Robert Browning and Elizabeth Barrett*
Biographies Pages 596

☐ **Gleanings In Genesis (volume I)** by *Arthur W. Pink* ISBN: 1-59462-130-6 $27.45
Appropriately has Genesis been termed "the seed plot of the Bible" for in it we have, in germ form, almost all of the great doctrines which are afterwards fully developed in the books of Scripture which follow...
Religion/Inspirational Pages 420

☐ **The Master Key** by *L. W. de Laurence* ISBN: 1-59462-001-6 $30.95
In no branch of human knowledge has there been a more lively increase of the spirit of research during the past few years than in the study of Psychology, Concentration and Mental Discipline. The requests for authentic lessons in Thought Control, Mental Discipline and...
New Age/Business Pages 422

☐ **The Lesser Key Of Solomon Goetia** by *L. W. de Laurence* ISBN: 1-59462-092-X $9.95
This translation of the first book of the "Lernegton" which is now for the first time made accessible to students of Talismanic Magic was done, after careful collation and edition, from numerous Ancient Manuscripts in Hebrew, Latin, and French...
New Age/Occult Pages 92

☐ **Rubaiyat Of Omar Khayyam** by *Edward Fitzgerald* ISBN:1-59462-332-5 $13.95
Edward Fitzgerald, whom the world has already learned, in spite of his own efforts to remain within the shadow of anonymity, to look upon as one of the rarest poets of the century, was born at Bredfield, in Suffolk, on the 31st of March, 1809. He was the third son of John Purcell...
Music Pages 172

☐ **Ancient Law** by *Henry Maine* ISBN: 1-59462-128-4 $29.95
The chief object of the following pages is to indicate some of the earliest ideas of mankind, as they are reflected in Ancient Law, and to point out the relation of those ideas to modern thought.
Religion/History Pages 452

☐ **Far-Away Stories** by *William J. Locke* ISBN: 1-59462-129-2 $19.45
"Good wine needs no bush, but a collection of mixed vintages does. And this book is just such a collection. Some of the stories I do not want to remain buried for ever in the museum files of dead magazine-numbers an author's not unpardonable vanity..."
Fiction Pages 272

☐ **Life of David Crockett** by *David Crockett* ISBN: 1-59462-250-7 $27.45
"Colonel David Crockett was one of the most remarkable men of the times in which he lived. Born in humble life, but gifted with a strong will, an indomitable courage, and unremitting perseverance...
Biographies/New Age Pages 424

☐ **Lip-Reading** by *Edward Nitchie* ISBN: 1-59462-206-X $25.95
Edward B. Nitchie, founder of the New York School for the Hard of Hearing, now the Nitchie School of Lip-Reading, Inc, wrote "LIP-READING Principles and Practice". The development and perfecting of this meritorious work on lip-reading was an undertaking...
How-to Pages 400

☐ **A Handbook of Suggestive Therapeutics, Applied Hypnotism, Psychic Science** ISBN: 1-59462-214-0 $24.95
by *Henry Munro*
Health/New Age/Health/Self-help Pages 376

☐ **A Doll's House: and Two Other Plays** by *Henrik Ibsen* ISBN: 1-59462-112-8 $19.95
Henrik Ibsen created this classic when in revolutionary 1848 Rome. Introducing some striking concepts in playwriting for the realist genre, this play has been studied the world over.
Fiction/Classics/Plays 308

☐ **The Light of Asia** by *sir Edwin Arnold* ISBN: 1-59462-204-3 $13.95
In this poetic masterpiece, Edwin Arnold describes the life and teachings of Buddha. The man who was to become known as Buddha to the world was born as Prince Gautama of India but he rejected the worldly riches and abandoned the reigns of power when...
Religion/History/Biographies Pages 170

☐ **The Complete Works of Guy de Maupassant** by *Guy de Maupassant* ISBN: 1-59462-157-8 $16.95
"For days and days, nights and nights, I had dreamed of that first kiss which was to consecrate our engagement, and I knew not on what spot I should put my lips..."
Fiction/Classics Pages 240

☐ **The Art of Cross-Examination** by *Francis L. Wellman* ISBN: 1-59462-309-0 $26.95
Written by a renowned trial lawyer, Wellman imparts his experience and uses case studies to explain how to use psychology to extract desired information through questioning.
How-to/Science/Reference Pages 408

☐ **Answered or Unanswered?** by *Louisa Vaughan* ISBN: 1-59462-248-5 $10.95
Miracles of Faith in China
Religion Pages 112

☐ **The Edinburgh Lectures on Mental Science (1909)** by *Thomas* ISBN: 1-59462-008-3 $11.95
This book contains the substance of a course of lectures recently given by the writer in the Queen Street Hall, Edinburgh. Its purpose is to indicate the Natural Principles governing the relation between Mental Action and Material Conditions...
New Age/Psychology Pages 148

☐ **Ayesha** by *H. Rider Haggard* ISBN: 1-59462-301-5 $24.95
Verily and indeed it is the unexpected that happens! Probably if there was one person upon the earth from whom the Editor of this, and of a certain previous history, did not expect to hear again...
Classics Pages 380

☐ **Ayala's Angel** by *Anthony Trollope* ISBN: 1-59462-352-X $29.95
The two girls were both pretty, but Lucy who was twenty-one who supposed to be simple and comparatively unattractive, whereas Ayala was credited, as her Bombwhat romantic name might show, with poetic charm and a taste for romance. Ayala when her father died was nineteen...
Fiction Pages 484

☐ **The American Commonwealth** by *James Bryce* ISBN: 1-59462-286-8 $34.45
An interpretation of American democratic political theory. It examines political mechanics and society from the perspective of Scotsman James Bryce
Politics Pages 572

☐ **Stories of the Pilgrims** by *Margaret P. Pumphrey* ISBN: 1-59462-116-0 $17.95
This book explores pilgrims religious oppression in England as well as their escape to Holland and eventual crossing to America on the Mayflower, and their early days in New England...
History Pages 268

www.bookjungle.com email: sales@bookjungle.com fax: 630-214-0564 mail: Book Jungle PO Box 2226 Champaign, IL 61825

			QTY

The Fasting Cure *by Sinclair Upton* ISBN: *1-59462-222-1* **$13.95**
In the Cosmopolitan Magazine for May, 1910, and in the Contemporary Review (London) for April, 1910, I published an article dealing with my experiences in fasting. I have written a great many magazine articles, but never one which attracted so much attention... New Age/Self Help/Health Pages 164

Hebrew Astrology *by Sepharial* ISBN: *1-59462-308-2* **$13.45**
In these days of advanced thinking it is a matter of common observation that we have left many of the old landmarks behind and that we are now pressing forward to greater heights and to a wider horizon than that which represented the mind-content of our progenitors... Astrology Pages 144

Thought Vibration or The Law of Attraction in the Thought World ISBN: *1-59462-127-6* **$12.95**
by William Walker Atkinson Psychology/Religion Pages 144

Optimism *by Helen Keller* ISBN: *1-59462-108-X* **$15.95**
Helen Keller was blind, deaf, and mute since 19 months old, yet famously learned how to overcome these handicaps, communicate with the world, and spread her lectures promoting optimism. An inspiring read for everyone... Biographies/Inspirational Pages 84

Sara Crewe *by Frances Burnett* ISBN: *1-59462-360-0* **$9.45**
In the first place, Miss Minchin lived in London. Her home was a large, dull, tall one, in a large, dull square, where all the houses were alike, and all the sparrows were alike, and where all the door-knockers made the same heavy sound... Childrens/Classic Pages 88

The Autobiography of Benjamin Franklin *by Benjamin Franklin* ISBN: *1-59462-135-7* **$24.95**
The Autobiography of Benjamin Franklin has probably been more extensively read than any other American historical work, and no other book of its kind has had such ups and downs of fortune. Franklin lived for many years in England, where he was agent... Biographies/History Pages 332

Name	
Email	
Telephone	
Address	
City, State ZIP	

☐ Credit Card   ☐ Check / Money Order

Credit Card Number	
Expiration Date	
Signature	

Please Mail to: Book Jungle
PO Box 2226
Champaign, IL 61825
or Fax to: 630-214-0564

ORDERING INFORMATION
web: *www.bookjungle.com*
email: *sales@bookjungle.com*
fax: *630-214-0564*
mail: *Book Jungle PO Box 2226 Champaign, IL 61825*
or PayPal *to sales@bookjungle.com*

Please contact us for bulk discounts

DIRECT-ORDER TERMS

20% Discount if You Order Two or More Books
Free Domestic Shipping!
Accepted: Master Card, Visa, Discover, American Express

www.ingramcontent.com/pod-product-compliance
Lightning Source LLC
Chambersburg PA
CBHW080509110426
42742CB00017B/3052